CHANGING COMPETITION, STATE, AND SOCIETY

CHANGING COMPETITION, STATE, AND SOCIETY

Reinterpreting the Neoclassical Model

Andy K. C. Chan

First published in Hong Kong in 2016 by
Re-In Group Limited
www.re-ingroup.com

Copyright © 2015 by Andy K. C. Chan
Printed by CreateSpace, an Amazon.com Company

ISBN: 9881436605
ISBN-13: 9789881436603

For my dad and mom

Contents

Preface

Economics has become one of the most popular subjects in school. It was my favorite subject in secondary school and continued to be so in university and afterward. However, to me, if not to many others as well, it is a weird subject. Although it offers frequent references to daily life, the more advanced your study is, the more farfetched from real life it appears to be. For instance, it seems that one needs to be very clever, and meticulously so, to be an economic or rational man. The distinction between selfishness and self-interest is at best blurred. Benevolence requires incentives but is not necessarily out of compassion. Different sizes of firms or types of market structure are taught, but we do not look at their coexistence or evolution.

As for macroeconomics, teaching this subject often seems more like explaining why economists do not have an idea of what the economy is doing or where it is heading. Inequalities, among nations and among individuals, are somewhat a necessary evil, though it is politically incorrect to say so. Mathematical rigor, one of the most notable changes of the subject in the past few decades, does not look able to resolve such issues.

Of the anomalies (similar to the above) that came up during my schooltime, one was particularly troubling. In microeconomics, the "neoclassical model" maintains that in a market economy, actions of self-interest and rational individuals will result in the best possible state, not only for each and every individual but also for the society as a whole. Though it sounds harmonious, the truly harmonious scenario is based on an implicit assumption that each individual can refuse to accept exchanges that he or she does not like—that is, that staying out or sticking to the status quo is always an option. Only in this way can we have exchanges that are mutually beneficial, or at least nondetrimental, to all parties. That, however, excludes the many pursuits by individuals, groups, firms, or nations to harm other parties that can be so readily found in daily life and history.

This book attempts to revise the neoclassical model, using basic principles and charts, by taking out the status-quo assumption. Aggressions are thus permitted. The revised model is then expanded and applied to revisit and reinterpret the theories of consumer and market structure, and the role of state, as well as the neoclassical model itself.

As mentioned, accumulation of the ideas for this book started in my school days. Writing this book has taken longer than the longest possible time I could have imagined when I began. I have made it through largely because I did not track how long it was taking. Of course, this would not have been possible without the unfailing and unquestioning trust exhibited by my parents, wife, family, and friends in what I have been doing.

I must also thank several former colleagues who unknowingly supported this project by giving me a generously credited store value card for a coffee-shop chain, making the times when I did not want to work at a library incomparably more fulfilling and joyful.

Since it is pretty challenging for an author not working in or affiliated with the academic circle to publish an academic book, my thanks are also extended to the self-publishing services at Amazon.com, as well as to another former colleague who informed me about the availability of such services to industry "outsiders."

My hope for this book is that it will help narrow the gap between what is taught and what we perceive as reality for this interesting subject. Whether as an analytical tool or way of thinking, economics can be a very flexible and encompassing platform, particularly useful in conducting inter-disciplinary studies on the course, past or ahead, of human societies.

1

Introduction

Economics, simply put, is a study of human economic activities. It covers topics not only on the national and global levels—typically under the macroeconomics category and dealing with variables like national outputs, inflation, interest rates, unemployment, and exchange rates—but also on the individual and the firm levels for decisions on consumption and production, customarily grouped in the microeconomics arena. On top of that, the subject also covers topics like comparative economic systems and economic development in poorer countries.

Nonetheless, challenges on the subject abound. The profession as practiced is criticized for being unable to arrive at unified views or solutions to some seemingly very common economic problems, like how to put economies on a more secured growth track or ensure enough jobs for those looking for work. Microeconomics in the form of the individual optimization model is criticized for not being capable of providing useful insights to solving daily economic issues like traffic congestion and air pollution. On a more fundamental level, even after the collapse of state communism and the apparent triumph of market democracy, economists still cannot agree on how to alleviate poverty, not only in less-advanced countries, but also in the many developed economies. The issue of inequality looks increasingly more endemic than transient.

Some authoritarian regimes, in contrast, can deliver long streaks of growth on the market economy model with no signs of any credible competition to the political center. Ironically, democracies, established or infant, also can seldom bring successful and sustainable challenges to the incumbent factions, especially those with military backings. Even though the right to choose may be institutionalized, meaningful choices may not be.

Casual observations such as the above put the subject in an odd position. After centuries of study, the theoretical construct is still unable to yield convincing and effective solutions to issues of such basic nature and importance. This book attempts to develop a theoretical framework that can address the preceding issues by amending and reinterpreting the basic microeconomic model. To do that, we will first focus on the following four general anomalies in the model.

Firstly, in the standard treatment on market structure, it is asserted that there are four types of structures, namely perfect competition, monopolistic competition, oligopoly, and monopoly. These are generally classified based on the number of sellers in the market, with each denoting a certain degree of competition intensity. Yet the classification of the four market structures is discrete, and analyses on them are not linked or integrated. When analyzing a market-structure problem or conducting a competition analysis, for instance, one first needs to fit the case with the type of market structure and then apply the corresponding analyses to see what the results would be. However, are the four market structures interrelated? How might one market be transformed from one type to another, if at all?

Such questions carry not only academic significance but also extensive applicability to business as well as politico-economic analyses. For example, why would industries evolve from an initial stage of numerous small companies, many being start-ups, to a mature stage of a few large players surrounded by numerous small players competing for subcontracts or buyout offers from the former group, or facing wipeouts, or more likely both? Applying this to the political arena, why would a large empire break up into smaller states?

Secondly, the perfect competition scenario in the neoclassical model portrays an ideal picture where the pursuits of self-interest by rational individuals will lead to an end state where not only every individual, but also the society or the collective, as an aggregate of individuals, are at their best possible states, and all exchanges or moves are mutually beneficial such that no single party suffers during the process. As robust as this conclusion sounds, it does not bear resemblance to the large trunk of economic behavior and activities we observe or experience in reality, such as pricing strategies targeted to sweep away competitors, raids to seize goods from others, and wars targeted to destroy production capacity of enemies. Such aggressive and hostile propositions, with significant economic ramifications, are pursued hardly on the consent of the counterparties. Could such detrimental propositions be incorporated into the model? If so, would the robust conclusion and the neoclassical model remain intact?

Thirdly, the role of state, though imperative, is largely treated in the context of whether it is needed for the market economy to function well. The nature of the state is largely not tackled directly.[1] After all, even the question of "what the state is" is not resolved, despite the significant difference that the state could make to economic behavior and vice versa.

Finally, mainstream economics, especially from the twentieth century onward, has adopted positivism as its methodology and is concerned with the question of "what is" but not the normative question of "what should be," which is regarded as belonging to the domain of political or moral theorists. To facilitate the development of the model in the positivist tone, consumer preferences are represented by a given parameter set. However, with firms assumed to be profit maximizers and to produce goods that are expected to bring in the biggest profit, what the consumers want, especially the dominant ones, can determine the course that a society takes. That is true even for societies not organized on the market

---

1 Works in economics that deal with the role of state more directly include Y. Barzel's *A Theory of the State* (Cambridge: Cambridge University Press, 2002), which examines the effectiveness of the state as a provider of protection services and as a third-party contract enforcer, and the large literature on whether communism, where the state governs everything, works at all. However, the bulk of the related theories are about the state in a market economy and on parties trying to influence the workings of the state, like rent-seeking and interest groups theories, but not on the state itself. For a general discussion on the theories on the parties influencing the workings of the state, the reader could refer to D. C. Mueller's *Public Choice III* (Cambridge: Cambridge University Press, 2003).

economy model. Whatever the resource-allocation mechanism a society is on, the "contents" of the preferences of the individuals or groups that have the dominant effect on what is to be produced or consumed, and the strategies they take to pursue their interests, have long-term implications on the course that the community takes. Does a dictator intend hardships on his or her subjects? Do dominant corporations create business opportunities for the disadvantaged? Do the powerful kill or help others to fulfill their interests?

This book will develop a model within the neoclassical microeconomic framework to account for and resolve the above-mentioned issues. It first discusses the idea of individual propositions and the relationships of one's propositions with those of others, especially those of the dominant parties. It then examines the key elements of the neoclassical model as represented by the individual optimization construct, which is then expanded within the rationality domain by allowing the pursuits of propositions detrimental to the interests of others. As such, a large arsenal of strategic choices to harm others to benefit oneself becomes available. Propositions to seize others' goods may be as profitable as the propositions to buy the goods. Instead of taking the quantity of goods as the decision variable, an individual decides on the best level of spending to change the competition intensity to one's own advantage, which could be to fence competition or to foster competition, or a combination of both. Differentials in the effectiveness of the individuals' capabilities in fencing and fostering competition in turn have a strong bearing, not only on the success rate, but also on the strategies that each is to take and the resulted aggregate competition intensity.

Within the context of the developed model, we shall see that market democracy is not synonymous with effective choice. An incumbent dominant political party may stay dominant or become even more dominant when the society adopts a market economy system. Economic liberalization programs may lead to growth on the aggregate but not the individual level, and the majority of the poor might stay impoverished. In the political sphere, no party may be capable of staging effective challenges against the incumbent, even if democracy is introduced. That puts into context the question of why some nations can bring material progress to the majority of its subjects while some will not, despite their having adopted apparently the same institutional framework.

The developed model is then applied to the case of the state, which is assumed to be a self-interest rational entity and the most powerful party in the society but assigned the task of pursuing the interests of its subjects. The framework is extended to show the conditions under which it is possible for the state to carry out the assigned task.

The neoclassical model is reinterpreted in the context of the developed model. With detrimental propositions allowed and the status quo no longer an available option, rational behavior may not always result in exchanges that are mutually beneficial. The society may not move to a better state as a result of individual economic activities, even with no market failures. The robust conclusion as stipulated in the perfect competition scenario requires the fulfillment of some more stringent conditions.

To have a society where the members and the state act in a benign manner, apart from the correspondingly conducive institutional structure disincentivizing behavior that's detrimental to others, another possible but not necessarily incompatible route lies in what the members want as embedded in their preference set. Since what is wanted by the members can determine the traits of the community and the course it takes, if the members derive satisfaction not from or not only from taking and consuming goods but also from caring about what one does and what one does to others—where their preference sets are benign and embracive (such that their benefit-and-cost schedules change accordingly)—it is possible that members may bring their community to the harmonious state by themselves.

This releases the model from the general deterministic tone intrinsic to theoretical constructs on economic behavior using the "scientific" approach. Human behavior is not necessarily destined for any specific end state even under the deterministic working of the neoclassical model.

While the model is largely concerned with predicting what will happen under specified conditions and assumptions, by building different types of human traits into the preference set (the "contents" of individual preferences), the possibilities of "predicted" human behavior can remain unlimited. What an individual regards as valuable (and what not) is the free will of the individual. In this end the neoclassical model, though having its deterministic part, is compatible with the free-will stance.

2

Valuation Criteria, Harmony, and Disputes

In this chapter, we are going to establish a structure relating to an individual's views and the underlying valuation criterion, and the interrelationships between those of different individuals, particularly in the context of whether putting them together results in accord or dispute. Adopted criteria may determine not only what is right and wrong, but also, among other things, who gets what and how much. This helps in understanding the workings of an economy or society.

PROGRESS

One of the main themes of studies on human societies is progress. Generally, it represents a movement toward some ideal or destiny accepted as such. Yet different people may have their own notion of what progress means. Political scientists advocating universal adoption of democracy, for instance, would regard more and more people around the globe having the right to vote for their leaders as progress. Economists, typically more concerned with materialistic developments, would consider increasing abundance as progress. Sociologists who take crimes committed as a gauge of social well-being would take progress to mean continuously falling crime rates. Collectively, they would agree that a society with more people having the right to vote, growing GDP, and falling crime rates is making progress on multiple fronts.

From the above perspective, progress is a judgment on a subject matter that is basically anything that comes to one's attention, like GDP changes or local food safety, measured against some valuation criterion or the premise that one bases his or her opinions or judgments on, such as those subscribed to by the academics mentioned above. If a person thinks that a certain subject matter (e.g., more citizens being eligible to vote) is a development that brings an entity (society) closer to the ideal (full democracy) as conjectured by his or her valuation criteria (that full democracy is an indispensable feature of modern societies), he or she will be of the judgment that progress is being made in that society. Reciprocally, contrary developments that move the entity away from that are taken as regress.

Similarly, for the economists mentioned earlier, the subject matter and the valuation criterion would be the growth of GDP and that affluence is good, respectively. Mapping the criterion to the subject matter, they will be of the judgment that the entity is progressing.

TYPES OF VALUATION CRITERIA

The above subject-matter criteria structure can indeed be applied to formulations of many types of judgment, of which progress or regress is only one. When a different type of valuation criterion is adopted, different judgments could be made correspondingly.

Valuation criteria, for instance, could include accepted theories or knowledge that could be deployed to evaluate claims of what happened or new theories to see if they are "true" or "false." Based on the knowledge that human beings require oxygen to survive, you will assume that your friend who is telling you that he has been living without oxygen for a year is joking with you. Likewise, based upon accepted theories of aerodynamics, we can verify if a new fighter-jet design claiming to be less wind resistant can really rise up to the claim.

Some criteria, such as the length of one meter, are defined according to the number system. Based on those criteria, statements of measurements can be made concerning a subject matter in accordance with the applicable number system or unit scale. For instance, the statement "the wardrobe is two meters high" can be readily verified with some handy measurement tools, which are aligned with the corresponding number or measurement system. That is in stark contrast to statements based on some more controversy-prone criteria, like "abortion is right" and "capital punishment is just," where the validity cannot be ascertained by referring to some objectively measurable criteria. With the valuation criterion itself in dispute, it is not surprising that the debates on views spanning from such criteria are frequently mere proclamations of one's viewpoints rather than a search for the truth or even consensus.

COMMON CRITERIA

Nevertheless, does it follow that disputes could always be avoided if we based our judgments on some noncontroversial valuation criteria? Suppose you want to buy a wardrobe that can fit into your bedroom. Using a measurement tape at your home, you determine that your new wardrobe cannot be taller than two meters. Then you go to a furniture shop and find a wardrobe you like. You ask the salesperson to have its height measured. The measurement he gets using a tape in that shop is also two meters.

For the measurement taken at the shop to be dispute-free with your own, we need the following:

a) The parties concerned (i.e., the salesperson and you) to agree on which measurement tool is to be used (i.e., the tape), and both to have trust in the tool's reliability for the purpose (i.e., measurement).[2]

b) You to believe that the two-meter reading on the tape you used at home and that at the shop correspond to identical lengths.

Those two requirements are, in fact, grounded on the beliefs that

a) There is a criterion that precisely defines what the subject matter means—that is, the length of two meters—which could be

_____

2 Or you both have to trust the reliability of the measurement printed on the product specification sheet if one is provided.

commonly referred to by any parties discussing the subject matter (the common criterion condition).

b) The criterion has been adhered to by those claiming to be referring to it, which would include the manufacturers of the measuring tools used by the salesperson[3] and you in the example (the observance condition).

In other words, the credibility of a judgment (measurement) is derived from the credibility of the valuation criterion ("How long is two meters?") it is premised on. In cases of commonly accepted valuation criteria, the chance of these not being observed, say, by the manufacturers of the measuring tools, is usually too low to warrant a doubt, and hence the probability of a dispute over the measurement is also low.

THE EDGE OF OBJECTIVITY

Disputes over controversial issues usually spring from the fact that the parties are indeed subscribing to different valuation criteria and hence not fulfilling the common criterion condition. In contrast, criteria based on objectivity, like the wardrobe example above, make reference to natural objects or, more specifically, to the independence and regularity properties of natural objects, which are particularly useful in minimizing the occurrences of and settling disputes.

Natural objects are independent of what a person thinks or feels about them. They remain and behave the same under specific conditions no matter, for instance, who is taking the measurements. Such independence of natural objects makes human manipulation difficult to be tenable when those natural objects are used as the reference.

Take the two-meter example again. One of the definitions is the length of the path traveled by light in vacuum during a time interval of 1/299,792,458 of a second.[4] That obviously cannot be compromised by

---

3 Or this might be the wardrobe maker, in case the product specification sheet is taken as reference instead of measuring the wardrobe at the shop.

4 That is the more exact version from the earlier definitions like the length between two marks on a platinum-iridium bar designed to represent 1/10,000,000 of the distance from the equator to the North Pole through Paris.

individual efforts. If the specification were not independent but malleable by individual efforts, so that measurements taken by different persons give rise to different lengths, there would not be an agreed-upon definition of how long a meter is.

If the physical properties of natural objects, which are not malleable by human beings, were to change by themselves, the length of a meter would change as well. The regularity that natural objects exhibit—in the sense that we can be confident that measurements taken today and a year from now under identical conditions give the same physical lengths—makes the defined standard less prone to result in disputes. If that were not the case, it would be difficult to pinpoint an exact and fixed length that constitutes a meter.

It is of course costly and practically not feasible to verify if the accepted criteria are in complete accordance with the definition in daily life situations, but the trust of its eventual verifiability is sufficient to settle disputes in most circumstances (as in the wardrobe example). Those two properties of independence and regularity endow objective criteria with the properties of fixity and verifiability, which makes predictability possible, rendering them the more effective valuation criteria for preempting and settling disputes.

THE IMPORTANCE OF OBSERVANCE

The above, of course, hinges as well on if the parties involved are observing the criteria being referred to—that is, the observance condition being fulfilled. Put differently, disputes based on the same criterion would be from nonfulfillment of the observance condition.

Suppose you go to a marketplace to buy some chestnuts. The stall owner charges the chestnuts by weight, which gives him the incentive to cheat. For instance, he weighs the chestnuts using a pivot that can be easily manipulated. The setting would be set further against you if you are a tourist and the stall owner knows this, since the chance of your reciprocating against his cheating would be perceived to be lower. Naturally, your doubt would be based not on the accepted criterion of a kilogram or what constitutes a kilogram, but on whether the accepted criterion is being observed by the stall owner (i.e., whether the stall owner uses his own criterion of a kilogram to supersede the accepted one, so that identical weight measurement claims correspond to different physical weights).

If your faith on the observance condition being met is shaken, you may choose to assert your claims and argue with the stall owner. If you regard the deviance as insignificant, you may accept his offer without further argument. Of course, you could just walk away. What you would do depends on your trust in the stall owner's pivot and whether you expect it to be worthwhile to expend the effort to seek "justice." In other words, even if the common criterion condition is met, disputes are still possible if the trust in observance is low.

OBJECTIVITY AND DISPLACEMENT

Could objective criteria themselves be challenged and become untenable? The postulate that behavioral patterns of natural objects are stable and independent from our knowledge—meaning that the objects behave in the same way regardless of whether we understand how they work or not—remains unshaken so far. It is the interpretations or the theories as to how those objects behave that are challenged. Accepted theories then act as the dominant valuation criteria in evaluating claims related to the field, including new theories that have been put up to challenge the incumbent ones. When new theories are accepted as more valid, they would become the new valuation criteria in force.

That challenge process in the study of the natural world, now largely undertaken by means of presenting exchanges of ideas and associated experiments, could be costly and might even have been fatal in the past. For instance, Galileo advocated an alternative version of what the cosmos looked like, and particularly how it worked, that refuted the then-accepted version of truth stipulated by the Roman Catholic Church. He maintained that theories were to be evaluated against empirical evidence and by conducting experiments but not on religious doctrines. Despite his being prosecuted, Galileo's theories were eventually revealed, via empirical investigations and with reference to the objective matters, to be closer to the truth than the theories of the incumbents.

The church's dominance in explaining scientific matters and its standing as the criterion of truth was gradually displaced and taken up by empiricism. Theories on objective matters, whether from the church, Galileo, or anyone else, are interpretations or guesses put forward by individuals. No matter how long they have been accepted or how useful they have been in application purposes, they are still subject to challenge and displacement.

DISPUTES AND INCOMPATIBLE CRITERIA

Does the above suggest that disputes are inevitable when nonobjective criteria are used? The harmony among the academics referred to at the beginning of this chapter (who value higher democratization, quicker economic growth, and falling crime rates) suggests the contrary. Their criteria are nonobjective, which cannot be proven right or wrong with reference to objective criteria. But the academics agree on the verdict that society is progressing. Baring misunderstandings and logical errors, disputes are less likely when the parties base their judgments on the same criteria or different but compatible criteria, regardless of these being objective or not, and trust that each and every one of them in fact adheres to the criteria.

Suppose, however, that after some more in-depth inquiries, new findings as to the underlying causes of the developments have been released. The positive economic growth, as revealed by the new findings, has been attained largely by a regime that is totalitarian, which has implemented policies allowing exploration of mines by peasants who were forced out of their lands and paid only subsistence wages. Knowing this, human rights activists put up demonstrations to protest against those exploitative practices. Petty elections, as a gesture for higher democratization, are introduced at selected villages to pacify the activists. For fear of revolts, however, the regime has also enacted more stringent controls on local citizens to eliminate challenges to their rule, resulting in falling crime rates.

Some economists may regard that as the necessary evil in the development process. Yet if the political scientists and the sociologists in the example also subscribe to another more micro-based valuation criterion, which is that progress is to be measured by the well-being of *each* resident (in terms of, say, the nutrients levels taken in and the scope and extent of freedoms enjoyed by each of them) but not the society as an aggregate, the new findings may trigger a dispute on that new valuation criterion against the original three (i.e., democratization, material abundance, and crime-free, all measured on the aggregate level). The judgment that the society is making progress on multiple fronts has become debatable and controversial, if not wholly unacceptable. Disagreements have resulted, with the political scientists and the sociologists in one camp and the economists in the other.

Although the academics initially subscribed to different valuation criteria, they were in accord with one another. That was possible because the valuation criteria they subscribed to were compatible given the initial findings. The harmony falls apart when new evidence reveals that the progress is only on the aggregate but not the individual level, making the now relevant fourth valuation criterion incompatible with the first three and leading to the disagreements.

RESOLVING DISPUTES AND TWO NOTIONS OF ACCORD

Could these disputes be resolved? As just pointed out, disputes may be caused by the use of incompatible criteria. To settle disputes or restore accord, criteria leading up to the dispute would have to be discarded or modified accordingly. The ones remaining after the screening process then become the dominant criteria. At the limit, all but one of the criteria are displaced, leaving it the dominant criterion in place. Judgments or claims premised on the discarded criteria may hence be viewed as wrong when evaluated against the new dominant criteria, just like the church's view that the earth was flat became untenable upon the eventual acceptance of Galileo's theories. In the wardrobe measurement example, you could bring your measuring tape to the shop so that only one measuring criterion is in effect. Potential disputes can be avoided or resolved by employing only one criterion. All parties would, perhaps over a long span of time, agree that the new dominant criterion is better than the previous.

The debates among academics, however, illustrate the difficulty in resolving disputes when no common criterion that could be indisputably taken as dominant is available. Controversies thus caused are resolved typically by designating some criteria as dominant. That could be achieved by appealing to some discretionarily selected persons, like voters or adjudicators, or by some measurable criteria like the shortest time to complete a race when the dispute is over who is the best runner in the world. The involved parties may not agree that the criteria resorted to are the perfect evaluation standards, but they would likely have consented to the use of those criteria as the best or least-bad approximation or proxy.

While the above two methods of resolving disputes are consensus-based, disputes could also be resolved or, in fact, subdued by suppressing or preventing them from being raised in the first place. As indicated in the chestnut example, even though there is a common criterion (unlike the academic example where there is none), nonobservance makes resolving the dispute largely a matter of bargaining rather than seeking the truth, or a better approximation of the truth. An individual may or may not engage in an argument with the counterparty, which depends on his or her expectations of whether he or she could make a net gain by doing so. If the expected cost of arguing becomes higher for whatever reason, or the expected benefit is perceived to be lower (or a combination of both), the chance of pursuing an argument becomes lower. Still finding it disagreeable, one may walk away nonetheless or choose to yield to accepting the seller's criterion. Thus, disputes are avoided. In the yielding case, the store owner's criterion is used, regardless of its being true—or put differently, in observance of the common criterion—or not. In fact, by virtue of yielding, the store owner's criterion has become the de facto common criterion.

Each of us has our own valuation criteria that frame our judgments accordingly. It is not always that the adoption of different valuation criteria will result in disputes. It is the incompatibility of the criteria or the nonobservance of the common criteria, and hence the corresponding judgments (as well as them being raised out), that lead to discord.

If harmony is to mean the absence of disputes, which has resulted from members of a community choosing to subscribe to the prevailing criteria, we would have two notions of harmony. The first one is that the propositions of the members are compatible, including the propositions to accept a least-bad approximation, which results in there being no disputes. The second type is that the members find the dominant criteria not the best for their interests but still choose not to oppose the criteria because doing so is prohibitively costly, as in the chestnut example. No dispute is raised, or no resistance or opposition is staged. That, however, does not necessarily mean that the community is in harmony, which we would typically associate more with the first type of accord.

THE SIGNIFICANCE OF SOCIAL CRITERIA

Resolving disputes means that choices have to be made as to which valuation criteria are used to screen out the incompatibles. That criteria-screening process, however, also suggests that there is an underlying mechanism or criterion. At the aggregate level, the social criterion that decides how those choices are to be made determines not only which and whose valuation criteria and judgments are dominant (e.g., abundance in aggregate or for each and every member), but also how resources are to be allocated (e.g., the choice of which weight measurement criterion is used will decide not only the physical weight of the chestnuts you get, or the allocation of the chestnuts, but also the distribution of the money to be spent on buying the chestnuts).

It is therefore important to examine the social criteria that determine which valuation criteria are to be dominant in order to understand the workings of an economy or society. For instance, what brings forth a change in the dominant criterion (or how a criterion acquires and loses its dominance)? We will discuss in the following chapters the effects of social criteria on propositions, or the actions that an individual is going to pursue (and not to pursue), decided both upon the individual valuation criteria that one subscribes to and the social criteria one is subject to.

3

Individual Propositions and Social Criteria

AN INDIVIDUAL'S PROPOSITIONS

Each individual has many desires that he or she would like to be materialized, yet most do not expect that many of these will become reality. To determine which propositions or desire to pursue, individuals have to decide which ones are favored most and are the most feasible. To do so, one may rely on, consciously or subconsciously, some form of valuation criteria. This could be happiness, vengeance, money, or any other value standard that one may choose. Against the adopted criteria (which we term as the dominant criteria), propositions are screened, and the one chosen to be pursued becomes the dominant proposition.

That dominant proposition in turn functions as the criterion in deciding how to pursue the proposition. A teenager, say, may be enthusiastic about becoming a basketball player and may choose to pursue that as his or her career. Once becoming a professional basketball player becomes his or her chosen or dominant proposition, that teen may evaluate the various options and possibilities open to him or her and decide what and what not to do accordingly. The teenager may consult more experienced and knowledgeable adults for advice, undergo intensive training, join a suitable basketball team, or engage in any combination of activities that he or she believes is of use to that pursuit of the dominant proposition.

Choosing to go for the desire or proposition also implies what is to be given up. Activities deemed not relevant or less of a contribution to attaining the dominant proposition may be screened out accordingly. The teen may prefer, say, spending time on training than with teenagers who have adopted propositions that are incompatible. Using the defined structured meaning of progress discussed in the previous chapter, any developments that complement the teen's valuation criterion—that is, moving him or her toward the fulfillment of the dominant proposition of becoming a professional basketball player—are regarded as progress, and the contrary as regress.

THE NEED FOR SOCIAL CRITERIA

When contemplating what career to pursue (e.g., to be an actor, programmer, accountant, chef, entrepreneur, or politician), teenagers have to make similar decisions. Each teen needs to decide what and what not to do during the course of his or her chosen pursuits. When we aggregate the many propositions put up by each member of a community, we have a social collection of individual propositions. Evidently, one does not expect them to be perfectly compatible and in harmony. The basketball-aspired teenager may prefer his or her local government facility to be a sport complex rather than, say, a garden. Criteria on the social level determine which propositions are to prevail and which are to be rejected.

In a one-hundred-meter race, for example, the criterion that designates who will be the winner is the one who takes the shortest time to complete the designated distance, on the condition that the specified restrictions are observed or not found out to be breached (e.g., not testing positive for the use of forbidden drugs). In an auction, the criterion is the highest bid price—that is, it is the amount of money committed that counts. In a film contest, the situation is more complicated. Here, although there are general guidelines laid out by the organizers, the criteria are less clear-cut and objective. Subjective opinions of adjudicators play a significant, if not overwhelming, role. Besides the quality of the films, factors like the casts, crews, and prevailing politico-social orientations may also have bearing on assessments. With their discretionary power, the personal preferences of the adjudicators override the preferences of general-public audiences.

In the above examples, different competitions have different social criteria that determine which propositions are to prevail and which will not, and those social criteria have overriding importance over the criteria subscribed to by other individuals. The use of the shortest-time criterion suggests that slower runners are screened out, allocation to the highest bidders denies propositions of lower bids, and audience preferences incompatible with the criteria of the selection panel are to be negated. No participant has discretion over either the choice or the determination of the criteria. Individuals can only choose whether or not to participate, even if the predetermined criteria are controversial.

The above is not necessarily applicable to all cases, but we will focus on that type of scenario first and examine the effects of such social criteria on the value and the choice of individual propositions.

THE WEIGHT OF SOCIAL CRITERIA

What is the interplay between personal propositions and social criteria? Let's go back to the basketball-aspiring teenager. Two factors come to play in gauging the likelihood of this teen's success: 1) his or her relative excellence, and 2) the applicable social criteria. Relative excellence means how well one's excellence is when compared with that of others, which could have many facets. For example, how well does the teen shoot? Can he or she make three-point shots on a consistent basis? How about assists and steals? What is his or her average number of rebounds per game? More importantly, how great is his or her own excellence, however measured, compared with that of others playing at the same level of competition he or she is targeting? Moreover, since basketball is a team sport, how well does the teen fit in with the team he or she may be playing for? Will the teenager be able to excel in the role the coach assigns him or her and help raise the performance level of the team?

In other words, relative excellence determines the teenager's ranking in terms of ability. That, of course, is only one side of the coin. The scale of the teen's achievements, particularly how much he or she could earn in return, is subject to another set of applicable social criteria as well, which is the community's receptiveness or preferences concerning the teenager's performance and the sport in general. For instance, members of the community may enjoy watching and playing basketball very much, even if doing so requires them to pay. The players, especially the successful and popular ones, may be well remunerated as a result.

Engagement in the sport could also be enticing if it is used as a propaganda vehicle by a community's administrator or government, like the basketball teams in authoritarian countries. A comprehensive national program may be set up to train basketball teams to play for the pride of the collective in international competitions. The teams and the selected team players may, as a result, be generously supported and enjoy a more comfortable living than that of ordinary citizens, though the funding is directly from the government and not from basketball supporters.

Another possible scenario is that the whole community enjoys the sport but merely as a pastime activity. The members may play the game among themselves—but largely for leisure. Here, there are no commercially viable leagues. Individuals, as a result, could not make a living by playing basketball.

An even worse scenario would be one in which the government regards any gatherings among the citizens on whatever occasion as potentially hostile to its rule. Basketball games, if deemed subversive gatherings, may be closely monitored or even banned. Whoever is involved, especially those in a leading role, may be arrested and jailed.

The different scenarios mentioned above illustrate some of the different preferences and criteria that a community may adopt on basketball (i.e., as an entertainment business, a measure of national pride, a pastime leisure, or a subversive threat) and the corresponding implications on the livelihood of basketball players. Different social criteria determine who is to succeed and who is to fail, and stipulate different prospective scales of achievements and rewards that the participants may attain. Without the appropriate social criteria providing favorable incentives, even the most physically capable player may not succeed or may not become a player at all. If the teenager resides in a community that is not so enthusiastic about his or her proposition, he or she may revise that proposition, adopt another one, or move to another community with a more favorable social criterion. However, no matter what the teen's choice is on which community to be in or which social criterion to face, he or she is not expected to be able to replace or noticeably influence the social criteria by himself or herself.

THE SURVIVAL CHALLENGE

Other than the social criteria mentioned above, which are more a matter of preferences, there are criteria that an individual's efforts cannot tamper with for other reasons. One obvious example is that of physical survival. As living organisms, we need to take in designated substances in certain amounts to maintain life, such as oxygen, water, carbohydrates, and proteins. Even allowing for the inventories stored inside our bodies, survival requires continued consumption of those substances.[5] Since we cannot generate those substances by ourselves, we have to rely on external sources. That inability to survive on one's own, at least not so for the time being, puts human beings in an inescapably insecure position: our survival is not guaranteed but contingent on having access to external sources of those required substances.

From that perspective, the survival challenge could be taken as an inflow-outflow problem. By imposing what intakes we must obtain to remain alive, it constrains the spectrum of choice as to what we can and cannot do without risking our lives. We have to formulate propositions that would furnish us with inflows of the required substances not to be less than the amounts needed.

How is the survival challenge tackled? Nonhuman animals living in their natural habitat search directly for the foods and water needed for survival. Meat-eating animals, for instance, hunt for prey and avoid becoming

---

5 Inventories stored in our bodies free us from taking in the required substances incessantly but not indefinitely. For example, we can be without food for a few days, without water for fewer days, and without oxygen for a few minutes.

the same for others. That direct or hunter-gatherer economic mode was the dominant living mode for a large part of human history before it was phased out by agriculture. Although some hunter-gatherer tribes can still be found in remote places today,[6] the majority of humans no longer go out to the wild to hunt for foods or even grow foodstuffs only for feeding themselves. We now work to earn the means of exchange first and then use that to acquire the provisions we need for survival at a later time. For instance, many of those living in cities go to markets to buy foodstuffs needed using money earned from their jobs. With division of labor and specialization, as well as the feasibility of exchange, our living mode is transformed into an indirect manner.

Although the way we tackle the survival challenge has evolved into an indirect mode, the underlying survival criterion remains. It is just being met indirectly. The shift to the indirect mode, nonetheless, has made it possible for societies to entertain far more different propositions other than only those geared for meeting the survival challenge solely and only directly. It would be inconceivable to, say, the hunter-gatherers how much wealth could be amassed, especially when expressed back in terms of what was valuable then (i.e., foodstuffs and water), by being a top professional basketball or football player.

CHOICE OVER THE SOCIAL CRITERIA

The social criteria dominant at any given time determine, among the many incompatible individual propositions, which are to prevail and which will be discredited or discarded. As resources are apportioned accordingly, the social criteria in effect determine as well the well-being of the individuals making the different propositions. Although the collective ability of human beings to meet the survival challenge has grown precipitously such that the relative bearing of the survival criterion on what we decide to do

---

6 This suggests that the change of the living mode of a community, or the social criterion, is not an inevitable consequence of the age of a community or knowledge of the alternatives. In fact, it is more a function of the change of the scale of the community's economic activities that determines if it could afford or bring forth, for instance, increases in sophistication in living or transformations of living mode.

recedes, the incessant urge to get hold of more resources[7] hardly diminishes the importance of social criteria and its determination.

As assumed in the preceding discussion, when social criteria are predetermined, individuals cannot alter them, even if it puts them at a disadvantage. The choice is between submission and exit. In contrast, if the social criteria are changeable by individual efforts, a whole new vector of choice as to which propositions to undertake emerges. A change of social criteria will bring forth changes in what are regarded on the social level as valuable and compatible, and thus which individual propositions can prevail. One is therefore likely to be incentivized to support a change of the dominant social criterion to a criterion that is expected to be more beneficial to oneself. Similarly, a dominant social criterion that is more favorable to one's well-being may well provide him or her a compelling incentive to fight against initiatives to dislodge it.

The teenager, for example, upon evaluating the various options available, may regard being a basketball player in his or her country the best possible shot and decide to pursue that proposition accordingly. That is to say, complying with the prevailing applicable social criterion happens to be the teen's best dominant proposition. However, if he or she finds out that being a basketball player in another community is more rewarding, even after accounting for the extra costs that may be necessary, the teen may choose to leave his or her home community and move to a new one to be a basketball player there instead.

Yet if the teen's home community, for whatever reason, embraces the games more favorably, the payoffs to be a basketball player there may be improved. That is to say, if the teenager could somehow raise the local receptiveness to the game, he or she may not need to move to another place to make a better living. However, since the cost of doing so—say,

---

7 That urge perhaps is still out of the insecurity that human beings cannot self-sustain physically or, maybe even more likely to be the case, driven by greed as shown by the urge that is so evident among some of those who have acquired or inherited wealth already to the extent that expending additional efforts to earn more in order to meet the survival needs is all but meaningless (or any combination of the two or in conjunction with any other causes).

by launching a community-wide campaign—is usually large and the extra benefit accruable to a single player is typically small, it is not justifiable for an individual to do so. In contrast, it may be commercially more viable if the promotion campaign is conducted by an entity that collects benefit on a pan-industry basis and in proportion to the receptiveness of the game in the locality (e.g., a national professional association or a television network). A scheme design that is based more on the underlying beneficiaries often makes it more likely to be implemented.[8]

To further analyze an individual's choice, particularly over whether to passively comply or quit, to bend an incumbent social criterion, support an alternative, or even to replace the social criterion with one of his or her own (or the question of what makes a criterion the dominant social criterion entirely), we need to have a basic decision model. As already briefly discussed, we are going to use the "cost-benefit analysis" framework—a simple tool used in microeconomics—which we shall discuss further in the next chapter.

---

8 The denomination of the proposition, as typical in a monetized economy, is money. Of course, if the teenager is well-endowed in monetary wealth such that he or she needs not worry about having enough money for survival for the rest of his or her life, the denomination of that teen's calculus could merely be happiness or fun subjectively gauged on an individual basis. That is, would being a basketball player bring in happiness sufficient to compensate for the hard work required, or would being a basketball player be the happiest proposition among the various options he or she considers?

4

Cost-and-Benefit Analysis and Rationality

We will use the simple tool of cost-benefit analysis[9] to model how a decision is made. Its rationale is simple. It evaluates the worthiness of a certain proposition by comparing the value, however denominated, that is expected to be brought forth by pursuing it against the values of the alternatives.

SUBJECTIVE VALUATION

The first step, therefore, is to assign valuation to each of the propositions under consideration. Valuation is a subjective exercise and is relative and specific to the party making the valuation. For instance, the scenery as seen from a certain piece of land may be a beauty to the owner but to no one else on the globe. Or many may find the land so interesting that they are willing to pay a fee for a visit. We are concerned only with subjective values but not about ascertaining the intrinsic value of an object, if there is such a value at all.

We are also not concerned with whether many individuals have formed a valuation on a certain object and whether those valuations are favorable or not. What matters in the current context is that valuation is contingent upon the party valuing it.

---

9   This tool is a commonly used framework in microeconomics. An introduction on the topic can be found in any entry-level book on microeconomics.

The methodology used for establishing the valuation likewise does not matter if one is consciously adopted at all. For instance, accountants have some explicitly stipulated, though not leeway-free, methodologies to assess the worth of a business. Wall Street analysts may compute the same by referencing the accountants' reports and by using estimates from their own models or projections. Traders of shares of the same company may formulate their positions based on their own research or the research of others or both, as well as on perceived and projected market sentiments, price movements, and the like. Whatever the methodology deployed, what matters here is that a valuation is formed.

One could form a valuation on any object, or a ranking of valuations on the objects concerned, regardless of ownership of the object. Although by owning a property it is more likely for you to have a more informed understanding on that object, this is neither necessarily the case nor a prerequisite for making a valuation. For instance, a private jet pilot or engineer probably knows more about the operation of that jet despite the fact that neither is the owner. It is also likely that, for instance, the pilot and the owner have different valuations on the jet. Simply put, ownership and valuation are two independent matters. One does not need to own an object to form a valuation on it.

Unlike the computation of the amount of fuel required to propel a rocket into space (where the determination of the underlying parameters is beyond our interference or discretion and the accuracy of the estimation can be verified), there is no external and invariable standard to measure or validate the correctness of one's subjective valuation or the methodology adopted,[10] and there need not be one. You may have valuations similar to those of your friends or even identical to those of the rest of the whole world, but that does not necessarily make that valuation "objective" or "true."

By the same token, the search for the "intrinsic" value in investments—based on the notion that some objective valuation on an investment has

---

10 This should be distinguished from forming correct *projections* of the valuations on an object, such as with stock prices.

been ignored or missed by the markets—is in fact more about presenting investment stories to convince potential investors to put in capital so that they can benefit when prices of those investments move toward the "hidden value," "true value," or "fair value" rather than a search for the "truth." Yet, whether the "intrinsic" values could be uncovered depends on whether there is sufficient capital chasing the stocks, which is exactly the same dynamics for prices of a well-covered stock—indeed of any stock. With inadequate capital being put in, the "hidden" or "intrinsic" value remains "hidden." Similarly, an "overbought" stock may remain "overbought" for a considerable period of time as long as it is able to continue luring in capital. In short, there is no objective value in investments. Market values merely reflect the interactions of the subjective valuations of the parties involved, correspondingly backed by capital.

Some may assume that a collectible derives its value from its uniqueness. Yet if we include the time and the location of availability in the defining characteristics of a good, virtually all goods are unique. The gasoline available at a filling station on your side of the road is different from that on the opposite side and so is the fuel available now versus next week's. Also, Van Gogh's *Sunflowers* is as unique as a drawing by me. The huge difference in value derives not from uniqueness but in the subjective valuations on the two pictures themselves. *Sunflowers* and other pictures by Van Gogh represent some breakthroughs in the evolution of paintings and art. The appreciation of those breakthroughs leads to the high values placed on such paintings.[11] The high value of *Sunflowers* or any collectible springs not from the work's uniqueness per se but the valuations on the item itself.

EXPRESSING VALUATION

To express a valuation, one might claim that an apple is worth as much as an orange, or a one-week holiday package at a ski resort for your family about

---

11 The appreciation also does not need to be contingent on owning the art. After all, a key factor determining the significance of a piece of knowledge or work lies in its acceptance, which in turn hinges on the access, not necessarily to the genuine works but to replicated images. *Sunflowers* would not be able to command such a high value if it were not visually known to the world.

the same as a new audio system. Apart from equal preference or indifference, your valuation could also be in the form of preferring item A over item B (and hence, item B being inferior to A). Expressing valuation as such, one is in effect expressing a valuation in terms of valuation on another item, or making your valuations on the two items interlinked and relative to each other.

One may also assume that the video game covered in the latest magazine is more valuable than a collection of Adam Smith's writings. If you own the Smith collection and the video game belongs to your friend, and your friend prefers having your books to his game and you prefer having his game rather than the collection, an exchange at a rate of one collection for one video game makes both of you better off. To that effect, an exchange connects your valuation ranking, or relative valuation, on the book collection and the game with that of your friend, and the rate at which it is conducted is the exchange value.

The denomination, or how the valuation of a good is expressed, could also be in numbers, ranking, or any other type deemed relevant, which typically corresponds to the criterion applicable to the decision. For instance, if one is talking about market transactions, the typical denomination would be money prices. In a democracy, with the criterion being the highest number of votes, one would use the number of votes as the denomination. A one-hundred-meter race could also be subject to the same modeling framework, where the time taken to complete the race would be the denomination. Propositions may then be evaluated in the corresponding terms accordingly: money (e.g., the money a new business venture could fetch), number of votes (the number of votes that endorsing a certain position would amass), or milliseconds (e.g., the difference in the time needed to finish the race if adopting a new training program).

In cases where multiple criteria and hence multiple calculi are involved, we may need a common denomination for comparisons to take place. For instance, when nutritionists talk about the implications of different combinations of foodstuffs on energy intake, the calorie may be a commonly used denomination. Similarly, when discussing the feasibility of some multifaceted projects, man-hours may be used.

The choice of denomination would be less clear-cut when propositions involve denominations that are not directly observable and measurable, like satisfaction or happiness. We may think or talk about our conjectures in terms of that kind of denomination and assign significant bearing to them in many of our decisions, despite their being neither observable nor directly measurable.

A typical way to deal with such issues is to assign some observable and measurable proxy to represent that kind of denomination and assume the representation that links the proxy and the underlying denomination stable. A common example in a market economy is to assign money price as the proxy to measure preference, satisfaction, or happiness. The amount of money you pay for a good represents the amount of satisfaction or happiness that you expect to derive from it, directly or indirectly, immediate or deferred. If one is not to experience loss from an exchange or a purchase, being willing to give up a certain amount of possession (i.e., money) to acquire some other possession suggests that the acquired possession must be expected to bring in some satisfaction that is at least not less than what could be derived from the best object that could otherwise be acquired by the same amount of money. This makes that amount of money, which is observable and measurable, a proxy to represent the (minimum) amount of satisfaction that the acquired possession is expected to bring forth.

To make a valuation on an object, therefore, one just needs to evaluate how much of that proxy one would render indifferent to holding onto that object. If one deems an apple to be worth the same as two units of the proxy, one's valuation on the apple could be expressed to be of a value of two units of the proxy. With such a common denominator, expressions and comparisons of one's valuations could be made more readily.[12]

---

12 Continued ranking of valuations of items against the proxy like money gives a preference schedule in monetary terms. If the proxy is a continuous measurement standard and preferences are consistent, the magnitude of the differences in preferences expressed in terms of that proxy standard is made de facto material—in effect, converting the ordinal preference, where only ranking matters, into a cardinal preference, where the qualitative difference between the valuations also matters.

Now suppose that you have one hundred units of a common medium of exchange known as dollars and nothing else. Instead of directly exchanging with your friend, you find the Smith collection and the video game mentioned earlier both available at a hundred dollars each at a department store, which acts as a platform where the producers do not have to deal with the consumers directly. You maintain the same valuation ranking on the two items (i.e., the game is preferred to the book collection) and regard those two items as the most valuable your hundred dollars can buy. In other words, for each of the combinations of the rest of the items available at the department store costing a hundred dollars, you regard them as inferior to either the game or the collection. Your preference ranking therefore is the video game, the Smith collection, and each bundle of the other items that costs a hundred dollars.

Yet for you to make a purchase at that department store, the preference ranking needs to include as well the valuation on the option of holding onto the hundred dollars in the hope of buying something else at a different time or place, or both. If staying put is the most preferred option, you would not make any purchase at the department store. Otherwise, since acquiring the game is preferred to buying the collection, buying any of the other hundred-dollar bundles, or keeping the hundred dollars, you will buy the game at a hundred dollars. The exchange value for the game is a hundred dollars, as you in effect have exchanged your hundred dollars for the video game. Your choice of the game therefore reflects your valuation on it over the rest of the items costing the same, as well as the option of staying put.

An Objective and Complete Valuation?

As stipulated above, via an exchange, one is grounding his or her valuations on the goods to those valuations of other parties. If one of the items exchanged is a medium of exchange like money—which in effect acts as a common denominator—not only can expressing valuations be made more readily, but the measurement task is also simplified, facilitating interpersonal and inter-item comparisons as well as aggregation of subjective valuations. However, given that the exchange value is recordable and verifiable, does that make it an objective measurement of value?

First, the fact that a value is expressible in a verifiable manner does not suggest that the valuation is determined objectively or outside the subjective faculty of the parties involved. A record that is verifiable or an object that's observable does not make its underlying determination or operation mechanics objective or in compliance with the "laws of physics." How the earth moves relative to the sun in actuality and what we observe or conjecture are causally independent matters. Whether we subscribe to the notion that it is the earth that is moving or it is the sun that is moving does not alter the actual dynamics of how they move (or not move) with respect to each other—at least given our current state of knowledge that this is not so. "Knowledge," interpretations, or merely guesses on facts and the facts themselves are separate and independent matters. The "laws of physics" work as they do irrespective of our preferences, perception, or knowledge of them. Similarly, whether an exchange value is verifiable, or even whether an exchange has taken place at all, expressing valuations in monetary terms does not make the valuation exercise objective.

Second, the use of a recordable exchange value as the measurement of ranking tends to be imperfect or incomplete. The act of you exchanging the hundred dollars for the video game suggests that you expect the game to bring you a satisfaction greater than the best alternative that the hundred dollars can buy; otherwise you would not have made that purchase. However, if you regard the game to be worth $120, then using the exchange value or $100 as a measure of your valuation on the game is a measurement short by $20. Only when one is indifferent about the purchase would the corresponding exchange value or price be a totality measure of valuation. If not, there is an uncaptured portion.

Third, adapting a common proxy does not make the proxy an external and invariable value standard. Expressions of valuations remain a relative matter and are made relative to one's valuation on the proxy itself, which is still contingent on the individual's valuation. Basically, the more of a good that one has, the lower one's marginal valuation on the good would be. Thus, it is likely that the rich and the poor would have different valuations on money or the proxy, and specifically, the former would have a lower marginal valuation on it than the latter.

However, since aggregation on a common proxy embeds the parties' individual valuations on the proxy as well, for the aggregation of valuation of different parties to be meaningful, even when a common denomination or proxy like money is adopted, we need to assume that the parties have the same valuations on the proxy itself. Otherwise, it is similar to adding a valuation on an apple in US dollars to another valuation on the same expressed in pound sterling. Given that there is no guarantee that the proxy is valued the same by all parties, to sum valuations of different parties (even on an apparently identical denominator), one needs to assume the differences on the parties' valuations on the proxy to be negligibly small.

RATIONALITY

With valuations, we need to specify how one chooses. To add that dynamic to the model, we would deploy the rationality postulate, which means that a decision is deemed rational if it pursues a proposition that is expected to bring forth the highest expected value among the propositions being considered. As a simple example, if given the choice of an orange, apple, or peach, and assuming that all of them are free and a certain individual's preference ranking of those options is known (which in this case is in the descending order of peach, orange, and apple), we could predict, under the rationality postulate, that this person will choose the peach.

The rationality postulate is assumed held. This means that an individual will choose to pursue the proposition of the highest value among the possible options. By analyzing the preferences as well as the cost and benefit of the different options available to the individuals concerned, we could model decision making and predict individual behavior accordingly.

COST

If we regard cost as what is to be forsaken to get what one wants to acquire or pursue, it could be represented by the value that is expected to be derived from the pursuit of the given-up proposition. Similar to the proposition to be pursued, the value of the forsaken proposition is also defined in terms of the valuation one assigns to it. The difference between benefit and cost, therefore, is that the former is the value of the proposition to be pursued, while the latter is the value of the proposition to be forsaken. A cost concept as such leads to its common labeling as opportunity cost in economics.

Do we take the sum of the values of all forgone alternatives or just one of the alternatives as the measure of the opportunity cost? If it is the latter case, which one is taken as the measure of cost? The rationality postulate suggests that a rational individual always chooses the higher-value alternative until, of course, there is no more "better" available, implying that the best has been chosen. Since cost means the value that one is to give up for pursuing an option of a certain value, would the cost of choosing the best be the sum value of all other options? As only one option is allowed to be chosen at any one time, the choice of "all of the forgone options" as a bundle is in fact not an option at all. What matters, therefore, is only the value of the next best option that has been forgone but not the sum of all the forgone options.

Consider an entrepreneur who is contemplating acquiring a factory. If they are not used for the acquisition, the same amount of resources could be deployed for other purposes. Assume that among the other options, the one that is expected to deliver the highest gross return involves acquiring a portfolio of stocks and bonds specifically tailored to carry the same risk level as acquiring the factory. The next in line, requiring the same amount of money, is renovating the current office building, where the expected return, as mentioned, is lower than that from the portfolio of stocks and bonds. To simplify matters, we assume that the entrepreneur has the capital to pursue only either the acquisition investment or the renovation options; acquiring the factory means forgoing the expected return from *either* holding that portfolio *or* the renovation, but not both. The cost of acquiring the factory is the expected return from holding the portfolio or from pursuing the renovation.

Likewise, when one is given the choice of an apple, orange, or peach, choosing the peach means one is to give up the option of the apple and the option of an orange, but not the option of the apple and the orange together. The option of an apple and an orange as a bundle is never an available option. One is therefore only giving up the value of any one option but not the value of all the forsaken options summed together.

Only one of the forsaken options is taken as the measure of cost, but which one? Since by the rationality postulate, one is comparing the values of the different options so as to pick the highest-value one, we only need to know the value of the next best option to substantiate that the best has been chosen. The values of the options other than the top two, in fact, do not matter in the decision-making process as long as any of them does not overtake the top two. We just need to take the value of the next best option or the best forgone option as the representation of opportunity cost.

COST-BENEFIT ANALYSIS AND THE CHOICE

According to the rationality postulate, the factory is worth acquiring only if its expected return exceeds that from the next best option of holding the stock and bond portfolio. Choosing the peach is a rational choice if its value is higher than that of either the apple or the orange.

Setting the benefit or the value of the proposition that gives the highest expected value against the cost that is the value of the next best option (unless the best proposition is on par with the next best, in which case the net benefit becomes zero), we always have a positive net benefit for the chosen proposition, even if the chosen one itself is a negative-yielding proposition, as the next best would be an option that entails an even bigger negative value. Put differently, any proposition that gives a positive expected net value must be the best proposition.[13]

---

13 One may wonder, since evaluation is achieved by means of comparing the expected values of the various propositions, why bother with netting it against the cost to get the net value? This is applicable only on the implicit assumption that the pursuits of different propositions command the use of the same amount of resources, which makes the exercise about setting the opportunity cost of each proposition against its benefit redundant. However, in practice, pursuits of different propositions involve inputs of different amounts of resources, and hence the values to be forsaken or the costs are likely to be different. A proposition may bring in a larger expected benefit but at a correspondingly larger cost, yielding a net benefit that may be beaten by a smaller-size project. Although the notion of opportunity cost requires the cost to be expressed in terms of the expected value of the best alternative project that this particular amount of resources could deliver, for simplicity a common rate (which may be adjusted for size, types of risk exposure, or other factors that may be deemed relevant) may be used as the cost, especially in cases that call for explicit calculations on the values of the different propositions. Comparison is then conducted on the net expected values of the various propositions, and choice can be made accordingly.

Reality Check

Due to uncertainty or incomplete information, what actually results from the pursuit of a proposition may not coincide with what is expected. A proposition that was expected to yield the highest net benefit may turn out to be the worst. For example, the battles between open and proprietary standards, VHS and Betamax, and HD DVD and Blu-ray discs are only a few examples of the many contests that have taken place to become the dominant standard in a respective market. Those who eventually lost did not launch their campaigns to make themselves worse off. The loss may be caused by mistaken expectations due to incomplete information on the customers' perception or the competitors' cost structures. Or it may be due to an abrupt change in risk averseness in credit markets such that rivalry time is shortened to the disadvantage of one side, which would likely be the more leveraged one but in possession of a more sophisticated product. What matters to the decision-making process are not only the expected values of revenues and cost, but also the expected probabilities of the different scenarios, including that of losing.[14]

Mistakes may also be a result of one's persistent reliance on models that do not stand the test of statistics or some objective appraisals for decision making. This can be due to the cost of adopting the objectively more accurate and more sophisticated models (which is prohibitively costly for an individual), or for some subjective stubbornness like the belief that one's methodology is to beat the objective odds eventually. It could also be a case where a person gets nonmonetary benefit from making otherwise unwise outlays.

For instance, one may find it exciting to bet aggressively on the unlikely or exceedingly rewarding to bet excessively conservatively. This is indeed applicable to benevolent activities as well, as one may be happy

---

14 This probability-adjusted decision making could be exemplified by applying the model to the decision of whether to buy a travel insurance policy for a leisure trip. You may evaluate that by comparing the policy's expected benefit, which could be the sum of compensations spelled out in the policy adjusted for the expected chance of their becoming applicable (plus the value of the peace of mind or any other benefits, if any, from having bought the policy), against the expected cost as represented by the insurance premium.

knowing others are being helped by his or her efforts. The happiness could be measured by the expected extra loss on betting against the established odds in cases of irrational betting, or in the amount of donations in cases of benevolence.

One must note that the psychological well-being or the actual cognitive criteria deployed by an individual when making a decision is not what the model focuses on. As far as the purpose of this analysis is concerned, there need not be a restriction on the type or the denomination of the criterion deployed by the individual, and it is not required that decisions have to be right consequentially or that no mistakes are made. Smartness, statistical correctness, or any other type of merit does not necessarily constrain what one chooses. More probably, they constrain what one gets. After all, mistaken decisions, made for whatever reason, carry a price, and one has to bear the associated losses. How long or how much loss one can sustain depends on the size of his or her endowment and incomes, just like one cannot donate beyond his or her means. The model is only about an individual taking the proposition that he or she subjectively deems best based on his or her evaluation.

TO CHANGE THE SOCIAL CRITERION?

Although a proposition to change a social criterion usually calls for a larger-scale effort and involves a group of individuals, the rationale for deciding whether to organize or support a replacement of the dominant social criterion remains the same: to pursue the proposition that is expected to yield the highest benefit. That is to say, an individual needs to consider whether the benefit that is expected to be obtained from organizing or supporting the putting-up of a new social criterion is greater than the highest of, say, that of supporting a failed replacement effort (or that of staying put if the replacement effort succeeds, or of staying put if the effort fails), adjusted for the corresponding expected chances of success.

Since a change of the social criteria would lead to a change in the corresponding costs and benefits to the individuals concerned, a complete replacement of social criteria means a corresponding redrawing of the winner-loser map. It is therefore likely that such changes of social criteria would be advocated by the most incentivized for the change: those who would be able to assert dominance in the new landscape—like the French Empire in the Napoleonic era, Prussia in the unification of the German states, or the Bolsheviks in the second Russian revolution.

Once a social criterion is successfully changed, sustainability of that change depends on how effective the new criterion is in luring subsequent allegiance to it. In other words, for a change to be sustainable, costs and benefits for individuals involved have to be changed in such a way that it is no longer worthwhile for them (especially those who have the power to revert or derail the change) to push for another change—rather, it is in their interests to support or live with the new criterion in place.

Resistances to changes may be bought off by offering benefit in excess of that which was offered under the old regime (e.g., lower taxes, or higher income or lands). Likewise, resistance can be undermined by forfeiting or chipping away at resources under control of the potentially hostile (e.g., land reforms or national movements to seize the property of former incumbent interests), by curtailing their coercive capabilities (e.g., stripping the incumbent monarch's command of the military), or by simply crushing them (e.g., the Russian revolutions).

A change of social criterion may not always be as extensive as those regime changes mentioned above. It could simply be, say, a change of the pricing rules you adopt for your online store. Instead of selling your goods to the bidder offering the highest price, you may decide to charge a fixed minimum price and sell the goods on a "first come, first served" basis in order to save the effort needed to conduct auctions. A new social criterion can also involve a new consumption theme that has become fashionable within a community, giving the associated products a price premium, which may even be inflated if the rising premium triggers further chase-after momentum. Reciprocally, given its subjective nature, as soon as what is fashionable becomes unfashionable, the premium vanishes and the social criterion loses its grip accordingly.

* * *

Using the cost-benefit-analysis framework and the rationality postulate, decision making can be modeled correspondingly. Whether the decision involves picking a fruit or a profession, or staging a battle against an industry giant, or acquiring a petty rival, the rationale remains the same: to choose the best-yielding proposition. In the next chapter, we will look into the implications of organizing a community on such a precept and see if it always leads to harmony.

5

Rationality and Harmony: Top Down

The rationality postulate plays a key role in the microeconomic model, as it stipulates the dynamics of how individuals decide and act. Simply put, the rationality postulate implies that a rational individual pursues what he or she regards as the best possible scenario for himself or herself. At any given moment, the individual either is in such a pursuit so that he or she is moving toward the best possible state where no more progress is conceived possible, or he or she is already there.

Does that mean organizing a community on the rationality tenet in which individuals pursue what each renders as the best for him- or herself is the best institutional arrangement, bringing harmony to all? Would rationality lead to different outcomes under different social criteria? For instance, are confrontations or inflictions of mutual harm possible? Would additional assumptions or restrictions be needed for a harmonious outcome?

To see if and how different social criteria under rationality would lead to different outcomes, we are going to compare and contrast the incentive effects on individual behavior first under the top-down planned setting, as exemplified by the communist model, and then under the free market setting, as characterized by the neoclassical model in economics. By doing so, we can see how differently individuals would act and where society would be led to under different social criteria—all assumed to be under the rationality postulate.

THE TOP-DOWN PLANNED MODEL

We can diagnose the top-down planned model by looking at its two components: "top-down" and "planned." A "top-down" society, as the name suggests, is structured on a hierarchy. It is run in accordance with the policies, commands, directives, or any other forms of expressions of preferences issued from the top. The line of command is from the top to the bottom, and that of reporting from the bottom to the top. There is no institutionalized channel to challenge the decisions of the top. Compliance is of utmost importance.

For the "planned" component, in simple terms it merely means that activities are to be organized or carried out in accordance with a preformulated plan. There is no restriction on the number or type of participants for formulating a plan or to whom the plan may be applicable. It may involve a nation, a company, a family, or merely yourself. Also, there is no prescribed manner as to either how a plan is formulated, or how the decisions over competing proposed plans are made.

Planning is not unique to the top-down model. It can be readily found in institutional arrangements not customarily regarded as belonging to the top-down specie, like private corporations in market economies. Management may designate focus products for the season; prescribe profit, market-share, or rate-of-return targets; or impose headcounts. While likely to be supported by corresponding incentive mechanisms, those "directives" are as expected to be attained by fellow staff as in a planned model.

Planning also constitutes, explicitly or implicitly, an integral part of daily life. We may have travel plans for work or vacation tours. The health conscious may follow carefully planned diets so as to control the daily intakes of nutrients, fat, calories, and the like. Plans are formulated and implemented regardless of the type of society or organization that one is in. Alternatively speaking, by making a plan for oneself or for others, one can hardly tell which specific type of institutional arrangements the plan maker is in.

The two components of the top-down planned model, other than being stand-alone entities, can also be combined with other apparently incompatible institutional arrangements. The examples of Chile under Pinochet and China since Deng Xiaoping demonstrate that a top-down political system can be combined with a bottom-up-type entity like the market mechanism. Democracies can also be mixed with a planned economy. War economies and, to a lesser extent, democratic countries with the bulk of the industries nationalized or extensively regulated, like France after World War II, exemplify that combination.

THE COMMUNIST EXAMPLE

As for the combination of "top-down" and "planned" components, it is customarily represented by the communist model,[15] where the Communist Party is the only social-criterion setter in the society. It determines, in the form known as "the Plan," what, how much, how, and for whom to produce. Plans made at the top typically become increasingly detailed logistically as they travel down the hierarchy. For example, lower-level comrades not only may be assigned production targets but also instructed on how the manufacturing process is run. The units at the bottom are largely responsible for executing some specific tasks that form a tiny part of the Plan.

Unbalanced Social Structure

To carry that out, the Communist Party establishes a special social structure to ensure that the Plan is being followed and complied with. On the one hand, the party has absolute power, owning and directing everything. It not only draws up the Plan but also enforces it. To do that and to maintain order and control, the party has the monopoly on coercive power.

On the other hand, to ensure that the Plan is executed as stipulated, the people are stripped of any power to pursue the otherwise. Consumption, work mobility, and geographical mobility of the subjects are all curtailed. Foods and other basic necessities are rationed, production quotas and jobs assigned, and shelters allocated. Essentially, no choice is allowed.

---

15 Karl Marx, although commonly believed to be the "inventor" of communism, did not stipulate the details of the communist model. His works analyzed capitalism, predicted its collapse, and portrayed a utopia of communism that would emerge after capitalism. It was the communist parties, largely *after* seizing power, that came up with the details.

Moreover, deviance is punished severely. For instance, subjects are forbidden to collude for purposes other than what is prescribed by the party. One may be imprisoned, sent to labor camps, or penalized, not necessarily for having organized or participated in subversive activities but for merely being associated, in some remotely related way, with a specific group or social class deemed subversive under prevailing waves of political upheavals.

In other words, in the communist model, to ensure that the party is the sole setter of social criteria, the social structure is bound to be unbalanced and decisively so in favor of the party. Yet, paradoxically, it is also that tilted social structure that eventually stalls it, as discussed below.

Persistent Errors

Given the scale and complexities of the work required for the formulation and implementation of the Plan, no matter how capable the comrades are, the tasks are practically impossible to be completed with satisfactory results. Mismatches of what is wanted and what is produced are inevitable, at least given the current state of technology. Stockpiles of unwanted goods, as well as shortages of many daily necessities, are common happenings. Queuing for hours is part of daily life. Worse still, poor planning by the comrades may even result in famines.

While planning errors are common and inevitable in economies and in daily lives, the incentive structure in the communist model makes the errors persistent. In a market economy, for example, entrepreneurs who have manufactured goods not wanted by consumers will lose money, compelling them to retreat or revise their plans accordingly. In contrast, in the communist model, as long as they are in compliance with the Plan, the comrades responsible for execution need not shoulder either the political blame or the economic cost of the errors. However, since the Plan is formulated at the top, reporting the errors may well be taken as a challenge to the top, thereby putting one at risk of becoming a victim in intraparty rivalries. In addition, the power to ration goods gives the comrades greater leverage in forcing through their will over the local subjects and hence gives them the incentive to neither report nor resolve the shortages.

Moreover, their ability to access resources first makes the comrades the last to suffer in material terms from planning errors. Given that the amount of resources at hand is fixed, to allocate more to their subjects to alleviate their hardships implies less for the comrades themselves. Given the people's repressed position under the unbalanced social structure, they can hardly pose a credible counterforce against the comrades to improve their quality of living.

The above suggests that where the errors lead to shortages, it is simply wishful thinking that the comrades will help resolve the problems, unless the shortages are so severe that the community is on the verge of revolt or a systemic breakdown,[16] or in the case that the comrades are altruistic as portrayed by Marx. In other words, the comrades need only manage their subjects to prevent them from staging revolts. They are shielded from planning deficiencies and also incentivized not to moderate the adverse effects of their errors on the people. Thus, it is the mass population that bears the bulk of the consequences of mismanagement and errors.

Constraints and Negative Incentives

With no apparent rewards but increased risks from reporting, and the minimal pressure exerted by people to rectify the errors and improve their well-being (all made possible by the unbalanced social structure), the risk and reward calculus in the communist model makes persistent errors an all-too-rational outcome. Yet except for the comrades and the very few chosen to work in "strategically important" areas, the majority of the people cannot be said to be at a living standard comparable to that of an average resident in, say, an OECD country. So why did the people not produce more than the required levels so as to supplement their rations and improve their well-being?

First, that may not be viable. Except for those goods that can be produced with labor power and freely available resources alone, it is difficult, if possible at all, to get hold of the extra resources or materials that may

---

16 This has been demonstrated by the experiences in China under Deng Xiaoping and in the former Soviet Union under Gorbachev, where reforms were not introduced until both regimes were on the verge of systemic breakdown.

be required to raise production output, as resources are allocated in accordance with the Plan. Second, products retained for self-use are vulnerable to confiscation or may even be used as evidence of being pro-capitalism or antirevolutionary. In fact, keeping properties beyond what is allowed by the Plan could be too dangerous a maneuver under a communist regime. The political constraint simply prevents one from having properties other than what's assigned by the Plan. Given the practical difficulty and the political constraint, enduring hardships would be the preferred choice over expending extra efforts to produce more to improve the well-being of the subjects.

However, from the comrades' perspective, some may fight for their own promotion by delivering to the top bigger volumes of output than their counterparts do. To do so, subjects under those comrades' rule or command would have to work more. However, as the amounts of rations given to the people are determined separately and remain unchanged regardless of the level of effort being put in, that means the subjects' extra efforts would not be rewarded correspondingly. Hence, plans to deliver larger output would likely be forced by coercion or other forms of negative incentive (e.g., by raising the penalties for noncompliance).

Moreover, the higher the levels of outputs that one is producing, the higher the level of compensation one would require for producing those additional units of outputs and the higher the level of corresponding negative incentives required to squeeze out those additional efforts at successively higher levels of outputs. In other words, the higher the level of output one is at, the larger the amount of negative incentives will be required. More and more resources are deployed for creating agitations rather than goods, resulting in bigger inefficiencies and wastes. That would eventually result in a net erosion on the pool of economic resources of the community, as evidenced by the general impoverishment of the communist countries running on the dogmatic communist model.

A top-down planned model necessitates the creation and sustainment of an unbalanced social structure. It is rational for the comrades to exploit the people on the one hand and for the people to comply on the other hand. The strict requirement for compliance with the Plan without the need to bear the liability makes errors, while inevitable, stubbornly persistent. The incentive system under the ideological constraints encourages the use of negative incentives and incentivizes the growth of wastes and inefficiencies. Inequality and antagonisms are systemic. Rational behavior under the communist top-down planned model does not lead to what one would regard as harmony.

Demise, however, is not inescapable. When the dominant social criteria change, rational behavior may change accordingly. As shown by the reform experiences in China so far, economic viability of the community can be saved by relinking the levels of rewards and efforts as well as by allowing the possession and accumulation of property by individuals without jeopardizing the "top-down" component by maintaining the dominance of the party against the people during the reform process. It is the "planned" component that needs to be rolled back and taken over by a more productive and effective arrangement, which in this case is the market mechanism.[17]

---

17 While both the Soviet Union and China tried to save the system from collapsing by introducing liberalization reforms, the different results of perestroika introduced in the former Soviet Union by Mikhail Gorbachev and the reform program launched in China by Deng Xiaoping have demonstrated the difference it makes when the party's relative dominance is not maintained when introducing pro-incentive or liberalization reforms to mobilize economic resources. The Chinese reforms, in essence, have released the economy from the ideological constraints of separating rewards and efforts, and disallowing possession and accumulation of property—thereby on the one hand releasing and mobilizing the vast amount of resources into economic activities and retreating the planned component, and on the other hand, more importantly, maintaining and indeed enhancing the dominant position of the Chinese Communist Party. The party's interests have been migrated to the more efficient and productive economic system, hence strengthening the well-being not only of the people but also of the party. This also explains why the various party factions eventually come to support reform programs. Perestroika, in contrast, gave more political powers to other political factions and the people without simultaneously strengthening the foothold of the party, especially at the center. It was also less bold than China in releasing the country from ideological constraints so as to unleash the economic momentum and gain stakeholder support for the reforms. The unfavorable dynamics of perestroika swiftly led to the breakdown and breakup of the Soviet Union, while the reform program in China turned out to be a hugely effective process for enlarging the absolute and relative position of the party in the country.

6

Rationality and Harmony:
Market Economy

The communist experiment turned out to be a remarkable failure. The Soviet Union broke down and broke up. China replaced the planned model with a market system and brought forth phenomenal economic growth. Equally humiliating is the affluence attained during the same period in countries organized on the market economy model. The communist experiment simply lies in marked contrast with the utopia portrayed by Marx.

However, despite the success in generating materialistic affluence, does a community organized on the market economy mechanism—typically represented in stylized terms by the neoclassical model in economics—also necessarily result in harmony?

Accord as discussed earlier is a state where everyone is happy in the situation they are in, or this could also be mixed, where some are discontent with the situation they are in but do not find it worthwhile to put up an opposition. Yet we would render only the first type of accord as harmony, but not the second where there is a mixture of two. The question, therefore, is whether the neoclassical model will bring itself to the first state of accord or the second. Since all exchanges are voluntarily entered into, the model carries the connotation that it will result in the first type where everyone is happy.

To see if that is so, let us first look at the several features or assumptions that typically characterize the neoclassical model:

1. Decision making is decentralized to the hands of the individuals. Each and every individual has the freedom to pursue his or her own propositions. For instance, an individual is free to choose what and how to buy or sell.
2. The rationality postulate is deemed held. Each individual prefers more of a good than less. Together with the scarcity assumption that resources are limited, one has to choose pursuing whatever option is regarded as most beneficial among all feasible options.
3. The realized value of one's proposition lies in the exchange value realized in the market. One sells in the market what one has (goods, services, rights, etc.) in exchange for other goods or means of exchange, which can in turn be used, directly or indirectly, to exchange for other goods at a later time.[18]
4. The benefit that one is to receive and the cost that must be borne correspond to the benefit and cost of one's actions, constituting the incentive and the disincentive or constraints for the actions.
5. Each individual has the freedom and the ability to refuse, without cost, to accept propositions that he or she regards as inferior.

The first point implies that it is the individual who makes the decision for himself or herself and has the freedom to do so, which is in contrast with the top-down planned model or other authoritarian regimes. The second one, or the rationality postulate, is the basic assumption made regarding the behavior of an individual. The third denotes the institutional arrangement of the market economy, where activities are conducted via the market in form of exchanges. The fourth assumption

---

18 The satisfaction or utility one derives from consuming a good could be more than what one pays or gives up, as represented by the exchange value, for the good.

stipulates not only the benefit and cost-appropriation rule of the market economy, but also the underlying philosophy that one is responsible and rewarded for what one does. The last one is usually not mentioned explicitly but, as we shall see shortly, represents an indispensable element to the argument that all exchanges are voluntarily entered into and mutually beneficial.

Putting the above assumptions together, if someone wants to acquire a good not belonging to himself or herself, he or she needs to know the preferences of those in possession of it and decide if he or she can and wants to meet their preferences on what to exchange for it. Similarly, others may also offer that person what they believe it is worth exchanging for.

That makes the social criterion in a market mechanism primarily about meeting the preferences of others in order to exchange for what one prefers having. A car manufacturer needs to know what car buyers want and the prices they are willing to pay for the car. A café owner needs to know the coffee and related preferences (i.e., the whole coffee experience), as well as the budget considerations, of those who may visit the shop. That links the preferences and purchase abilities of oneself and other market participants together, and establishes exchange as a key social activity in the community.

Harmony?

Is a community organized as above necessarily a harmonious one? Since each individual knows best what he or she wants, he or she is the best judge on what is specifically valuable to him or her. On the corresponding cost-and-benefit combinations, that individual will pursue what he or she regards as the best among the feasible options. With the ability to reject inferior propositions from others, for one to be willing to accept a proposition from another party, it has to be a beneficial one—or at least not detrimental to him or her. Reciprocally, for others to accept one's proposition, it has to be beneficial or not detrimental to them as well.

Putting this all together, exchanges are hence nondetrimental at the very least and mutually beneficial in general. In aggregate, a community organized as such will have its members on continuous searches for propositions that are expected to benefit one or more than one member, thereby moving the collective to the best possible state and, in a dynamic perspective, pushing the best to be better. The community is built on consent and is thus destined for harmony.

An Example of Exchange

To establish a further understanding of the workings of the neoclassical model, let us look at a typical two-person exchange scenario. It is assumed that there are two individuals, each possessing only one good. Each has his or her own and possibly different valuations on those goods. Let us assume that Person A values Good X at $100 and Good Y at $150. Person A owns Good X, while Good Y is owned by Person B, who values her Good Y merely at $120 but values the Good X that Person A owns at $150. Given such valuations, it is mutually beneficial for them to exchange their possessions. Person A trades away his Good X that is of a value of $100 to him for Good Y that he assigns a $150 valuation to pocket a value gain of $50 ($150 – $100). Person B exchanges her Good Y, which she values at only $120, with Person A for the Good X, which is of $150 value to her, netting a gain of $30 ($150 – $120).

The community, as a summation of the individuals, also moves from the original state where the sum of valuations equals $220 ($100 + $120) to a better state of $300, gaining $80 in aggregate (gains of Persons A and B = $50 + $30), illustrating the neoclassical model's argument that a community built upon voluntary exchanges among individuals is always on the move to the best possible state for each of its members and, as a result, itself as a whole, if not already at that state.

Scenario #1 in table 6.1 below recaps the preceding case.

Table 6.1. Preference Matrix

	Good	Person A	Person B	Outcomes
Scenario #1	X	$100	$150	Pursue exchange: Good X from Person A to Person B; Good Y from Person B to Person A; Person A gains $50 in value; Person B gains $30. The community gains from an aggregate value of $220 to $300.
	Y	$150	$120	
Scenario #2	X	$100	$150	Exchange if compensated: Good X from Person A to Person B, and Good Y from Person B to Person A only if Person A is compensated for an amount ranging from $20 to $30. The community gains $10 (from $220 to $230).
	Y	$80	$120	
Scenario #3	X	$100	$95	No voluntary deal is possible; the community also has not moved to a worse situation.
	Y	$80	$85	

Compensation

Suppose that prior to exchanging the goods, Person A changes his valuations, with that on Good X remaining at $100 but that on Good Y dropping to only $80 (Scenario #2 in table 6.1). With such a valuation mix, he would prefer keeping his Good X rather than trading it away, as the latter option will result in a loss in value of $20 ($80 – $100) to him.

The reluctance of Person A to exchange makes Person B, with unchanged valuations, unable to make the potential $30 gain. The community is also prevented from taking on the potential $10 net-value improvement (a $30 gain to Person B against the $20 loss to Person A, should the trade go through). As a person in the neoclassical model can refuse taking a trade that is detrimental to him or her (as will Person A in the current scenario), Person B, in order to induce Person A to go with the trade, needs to compensate him for his loss from the exchange.

Intuitively, we can see that the size of the compensation needs to be at least the amount of the loss that Person A will suffer should the exchange be executed, which amounts to $20 as mentioned ($80 – $100). For Person B, since the potential gain for her from the exchange is $30, she will be willing to pay a compensation only if it is not greater than that amount. A credible compensation therefore will be in the range of $20 (so the amount is just enough to make the exchange indifferent to Person A, with the whole of the residual gain to go to Person B) to $30 (so the amount is just enough to make the exchange indifferent to Person B, with all the net gain going to Person A).

No matter what the exact amount of the compensation is, as long as the exchange is made, the community gains from the aggregate valuation of $220 to $230, realizing a net improvement of $10. The size of the compensation makes a difference only to the distribution of the gain, but not to the size of the aggregate or social gain.[19] Nevertheless, the possibility of compensation widens the scope of betterment for individuals and the community.

Socially Detrimental Exchanges

Now, suppose that the valuations of Person B also change: Good X at $95 only and Good Y (which she owns) at $85 (Scenario #3). The maximum potential gain from the exchange to Person B therefore shrinks to $10 ($95 – $85), which is insufficient to compensate for the potential loss of Person A if the exchange is carried out ($80 – $100 = –$20).

Nonetheless, since Person A does not have to suffer a loss of value of $20, which is greater than the potential gain of $10 to Person B, the community as a whole avoids a change that would result in a net aggregate loss

---

19 Given that the gain made by Person B ($30) is more than the loss to Person A ($20), as long as Person B manages to get the trade through, the community gains a value of $10, regardless of the level of compensation she pays to Person A. That remains so even if Person B does not honor her promise of paying the compensation. The community still moves to the same equilibrium. That may be taken as the justification for dictatorships or letting the "strong hands" or the "wise" control the resources, since whether the interests of the weak are taken care of may not make a difference to the aggregate level of well-being. Indeed, not worrying about Person A's interests may even save the extra costs of arranging the compensation, enlarging the possibilities and size of gain. That is to say, a community may be brought to the equilibrium by coercion, in turn suggesting the incentive for dictatorships.

of $10 in value $10 – $20). The "failure" of exchange is hence preferred from the social point of view, despite the fact that Person B could not have moved to a higher level of well-being for herself (a gain of $10).

Incentive to Cheat

For the compensation to be credible, as in Scenario #2, several implicit assumptions have to be made. First, it has to be assumed that making the compensation is viable in a practical sense. For instance, the payment may have to be made in a fraction of either good, or a combination of fractions of the goods, that corresponds to the agreed amount of compensation. That may pose a problem if the goods are indivisible or derive their value in wholeness but not fraction, like a pair of shoes. In an economy where the medium of exchange is more divisible, like our monetized economy, the divisibility problem can be resolved more readily.

The second assumption is that the act of compensation itself is not prohibitively costly. More precisely put, the cost of making and securing the compensation is not to be greater than the gain from exchange. Otherwise, letting the exchange opportunity pass may be the preferred choice. For example, suppose that a factory is polluting neighboring areas and is legally liable for the damages. However, if the costs to ascertain the losses are to be borne by the victims, it may well be rational for them to give up seeking compensation if the expected costs of identifying the polluter, ascertaining the loss, and carrying out any other activities that may be required to make the claim exceed the expected amount of compensation.

The third assumption is that the exchange and the compensation are bound together. As shown in Scenario #2, it is rational for Person A to reject exchanging his Good X for Good Y, as that will cause him to suffer a loss of value of $20 ($80 – $100). Only with a compensation for at least the amount of his loss would it be rational for him to trade with Person B. It is therefore imperative for Person A to ensure that the exchange and the compensation are bound together, and that both are executed such that the trade will not become a loss to him.

However, that may not be what Person B has in mind. As depicted above, as long as there is gain to be made from the exchange (i.e., $150 – $120 =

$30) and if the compensation is less than that gain, it is in Person B's interests to pay the compensation so as to induce Person A to exchange, as she can still pocket a net gain that equals the gain of exchange less the amount of compensation. However, if she can evade paying the compensation but still execute the trade, her gain will be the gain of exchange without deducting the compensation ($30). That larger gain gives her the prima facie incentive to cheat on paying the compensation.[20] If indeed she could do that and cheat on paying the compensation, and could do so at a cost that is less than the benefit of cheating (i.e., the compensation itself), she is incentivized to cheat.

Cost of Cheating

So what would constitute the cost of cheating on the compensation payment? The first component is the logistics cost, which may include the costs of making the exchange and the compensation separate, as well as that of arranging and executing the cheat. The cheater may do so by separating the payments of the purchase consideration and compensation by making them in different forms (e.g., a combination of a good and cash), at different times (e.g., a combination of bushels available now and in the next harvest, or delivery in separate batches). Or the cheater might use fraudulent means of payment or records, like forged cash, delivery orders, shipment records, or any other "evidence" used to convince the counterparty that the cheat is anything but a cheat. Generally speaking, a typical cheat is likely to be where authenticity cannot be immediately validated or substantiated, which is why the cheater may separate paying for the purchase and the compensation.

The second component of the cost of the compensation cheat is the liability payment that Person A may be able to exact from Person B after being cheated. That is, after Person B has successfully cheated on paying the promised compensation, what subsequent liability payment, if any, could Person A get from her?

A number of methods can be used to seek a liability payment. For instance, Person A may sue Person B to recoup his loss, or he may take laws into his hands by taking revenge on Person B, who may as a result be

---

20 To do that she may first need to, in one way or another, separate the payments of the purchase consideration and the compensation.

willing to pay a liability payment to avoid being attacked. No matter which method is deployed, the ability of Person A to inflict damage on Person B shrinks the size of gain from cheating that may be available to the latter, hence reducing the incentive to cheat.

In sum, if the cost of cheating on the compensation, which is the sum of the logistics cost and the liability payment that is to be paid, exceeds the benefit of cheating (which is simply the compensation payment itself), it is rational for Person B to pay the compensation upfront and not to cheat.

Decision to Cheat

We could recap the above in the three scenarios shown in table 6.2 below, where it is assumed that the exchange and the payment of the compensation can be separated with logistics cost amounting to $5 in all scenarios. The benefit of cheating on the compensation is simply the amount of the compensation saved, which is assumed to be at $20.

In Scenario #4, Person A chooses to sue Person B, but he can only obtain a liability payment of $5. The total cost of not paying the compensation (i.e., the sum of the logistics cost and the liability payment) amounts to $10 to Person B. That is less than the size of the compensation cheated ($20), giving her the incentive to cheat accordingly.

Table 6.2. Person B: Decision to Cheat on Paying the Compensation

	Scenario #4	Scenario #5	Scenario #6
Benefit of cheating on the compensation payment (i.e., the amount of the compensation)	$20	$20	$20
Cost of cheating			
- Logistics cost	$(5)	$(5)	$(5)
- Liability payment			
> Legal means	$(5)	-	-
> Damage that could be inflicted by Person A on Person B by means of retaliatory attacks	-	$(10)	$(30)
Total	$(10)	$(15)	$(35)
Net benefit/(loss) from cheating	$10	$5	$(15)
Decision: To cheat?	Yes	Yes	No

In both Scenario #5 and Scenario #6, instead of pursuing the legal means, Person A chooses to deploy some direct offensive tactics. In Scenario #5, Person A is able to inflict a loss of $10 on Person B. Despite the damage, Person B can still pocket a positive, though smaller, net gain of $5, incentivizing her to cheat. It is in Scenario #6 where Person A is able to inflict a damage on Person B that is large enough to make her suffer a net loss that's enough to deter Person B from cheating and forcing her to pay the compensation.

To Seize?

If cheating on the compensation could be profitable, how about other means of benefiting at the expense of others? After all, damage-oriented strategies are not limited to cheating on the compensation. It could involve cheating on the whole exchange or outright seizing the good from others. Those strategies may even be more profitable than cheating on the compensation only. Analyses on those means can be conducted using the same framework for the compensation cheat, as they are highly similar in nature. In fact, they differ only in a matter of degrees. Let us see how that is the case.

Every exchange or transaction can be viewed as a combination of two component transfers: the transfer of the good itself (the good component) and the transfer of the payment consideration (the payment component). A buyer takes the good from the seller (the good component) and pays the purchase consideration to the seller (the payment component) in return. The payment could be in many forms, like another good or a common medium of exchange such as money. Cheating on the whole exchange could therefore be viewed as carrying out the first component (i.e., taking the good from the counterparty) but cheating on the second component (i.e., not paying the consideration in effect). Seizing a good from the seller involves executing the good component but not the payment component. The good components in the two types of cheat are the same; the difference lies only in the method of not carrying out the payment component.

For the cheat on compensation, the consideration component is composed of two parts, the purchase consideration and the compensation, and the cheat is on the latter. That is to say, the compensation cheat involves not honoring the entire payment component, while seizing a good from another party or cheating on the whole payment is a total cheat on that component.

Given the similarity, we could simply substitute the benefit and cost of compensation by those of seizing into the analytical framework in table 6.2, as is done in table 6.3 below. As illustrated in Scenario #7, Person B takes in a gain of $95 by seizing Good X from Person A, who suffers a total loss of $100 (the value of Good X to him). Although that will lead to a loss of $5 to the community and a loss of $100 to Person A, as long as the cost to Person B of seizing is smaller than the gain seized (i.e., $95), it serves as the incentive for her to seize the good from Person A, resulting in a net loss for the community.[21]

Table 6.3. To Seize?

	Good	Person A	Person B	Outcomes
Scenario #7	X	$100	$95	Person B seizes Good X from Person A, thereby gaining $95 (from $85 to $180); Person A loses $100
	Y	$80	$85	in value (from $100 to $0). The community in aggregate loses $5 in value: from $185 (= $100 + $85) to $180 (= $85 + $95).
Scenario #8	X	$100	$95	It could also be Person A who is the aggressor: Person A seizes Good Y from Person B. Person B
	Y	$80	$85	loses $85 in value (from $85 to $0); Person A gains $80 (from $100 to $180). The community loses $5 in value (from $185 to $180).

To Reclaim the Loss?

As in the preceding discussion on whether to reclaim the loss, Person A may not be a passive victim who stands aside and does not retaliate. Indeed,

---

21 This illustrates the case where Person B, or a dictator to the same effect, engineers a change that benefits only herself but at a loss to the community. Dictatorships warrant only the betterment of the dictators themselves but not the society as a whole.

what he is going to do could have a significant bearing on what Person B pursues. A key consideration is that after being cheated or having his good seized, will Person A make any offensive maneuvers to recoup his loss? Again, to do that, the reclaim proposition has to be positive-yielding to him, so that the liability payment expected to be secured exceeds the projected cost of reclaiming. Carrying out the offensive could be commissioned to a third party, which could be a justice administrator (i.e., suing Person B) or mercenaries and the like, or conducted by himself (e.g., waging a military campaign or a price war, or terminating trading relationships with Person B in the future),[22] with each option carrying its own combination of cost and benefit.

Within the cost-and-benefit-analysis framework and barring the possibility of altruism where Person B suddenly repents and pays Person A back, for Person B not to cheat or seize, or to agree to pay a liability payment to Person A after doing so, she is either threatened with a bigger loss due to consequences or enticed by a larger benefit.[23]

Therefore, these are the main possibilities: Person A simply seizes the good back or other goods from Person B; Person B is convinced of the ability and determination of Person A to do that, precipitating her to yield before the launch of the offensive by Person A so as to avoid suffering the expected casualties; or Person B is convinced after suffering initial damage from Person A's offensives, yielding swiftly to avoid experiencing further loss.

Since what matters to Person A is the reparations and liability payments that Person B is willing to make in order to avoid damage being inflicted on her (rather than the damages inflicted on Person B), the benefit of launching strikes is more uncertain than the value of, say, directly

---

22 Refusing to trade with Person B in the future may include not only the trades between Person A and Person B but possibly those between Person B and the rest of the community as well (e.g., the cheat damages Person B's reputation and credibility). The damage would therefore equal the sum of discounted net benefits of trades that would have been made in future if Person B had not cheated.

23 This is premised on the fact that the loss to Person A for being cheated is greater than the value of the cheat to Person B (i.e., Good X is worth more to Person A than to Person B). An example of such tactics would be a payment to buy peace.

seizing a known good from the other party. The size of the liability payment that Person B is willing to pay, while dependent on the amount of damage, may not equal the size of the damage that Person A is to inflict on her. For Person B not to seize or cheat but pay the consideration, she must be convinced that the size of damage about to be inflicted is larger than the benefit of seizing or cheating that she is contemplating pursuing, making it beneficial to pay upfront rather than to suffer the damage later.[24, 25]

Nonetheless, if none of the methods is expected to secure a benefit that could cover the cost of exacting it or even to secure a smaller net loss, it may become preferable for Person A not to pursue a reclaim for his loss but to tolerate it instead ($20 from the exchange without compensation, or $100 if his good is seized or cheated). In contrast, if one, some, or all of the methods are expected to put him in a position that is better than suffering the loss as a passive victim, Person A will pursue the reclaim and do so using the method expected to bring in the highest level of net benefit.

Some of the possible interactions are outlined in table 6.4 below. In the three scenarios, it is assumed that Person B seizes Good X from Person A, making the loss to Person A at $100, and the logistics cost of seizing is assumed to be $10 to Person B.

---

24 The outcomes depend on, among other factors, the size and distribution of the net damages, as shall be discussed later.

25 By the same thinking, Person B may downplay the loss she is suffering or is about to suffer so as to inflate the expected cost of the offensives that Person A needs to undertake, thereby disincentivizing Person A from taking those offensives. The dynamics could be made more complicated if Person B strikes at Person A in anticipation of or in response to the latter's launch of offensive tactics, further weakening the incentives for Person A to pursue the offensive tactics to reclaim his loss.

Table 6.4. Person A to Reclaim for His Loss?

		Scenario #9	Scenario #10	Scenario #11
To Person A				
Loss of good seized or if seized		$(100)	$(100)	$(100)
Type of reclaim maneuver		War	Administrator	Administrator
Direct cost of maneuver		$(50)	$(30)	$(30)
Threatened damage to Person B	$(60)		$(85)	$(150)
Liability payment (with Good X to be retained by Person B)		$0	$85	$140
Net benefit/(loss) of maneuver itself		$(50)	$55	$110
Decision: To pursue claim or not?		No	Yes	Yes
Net benefit/(loss) with loss of seized good included		$(100)	$(45)	$10
To Person B				
Benefit of seizing		$95	$95	$95
Cost of seizing				
- Logistics cost	$(10)		$(10)	$(10)
- Damage to be suffered and liability payment payable	$(60)		$(85)	$(290)
Total cost		$(70)	$(95)	$(300)
Net benefit/(loss)		$25	$(0)	$(205)
Decision: To Seize?		Yes	Indifferent	No

In Scenario #9, Person A chooses to threaten Person B with a war. The direct cost of that maneuver to Person A is $50. Due to Person A's inferior coercive capability, the maximum damage that he can inflict on Person B amounts to $60 only. Given that, Person B would rather tolerate the damage than yield, as she could still get a net benefit of $25 by seizing the good. However, as Person A is unable to secure a liability payment from Person B, he would choose not to launch the offensive after the good being seized, as doing so would only inflate his loss by $50. Due to his poor coercive effectiveness, the end result would be Person A tolerating his loss of the good and taking no action to reclaim that loss.

In Scenario #10, Person A chooses to enlist help from the justice administrator, which is all-powerful. The cost of that is assumed to be $30.

Despite the administrator's being all-powerful, the effectiveness in enforcing "justice" depends on the scale of punishment that is to be imposed on the "wrongdoer." If the administrator does not inflict a punitive damage so that the worst outcome for Person B is to be restored to the status quo only—so that to aim is to inflict a damage, or a combination of damage and liability payment, of $85, which is the net gain for Person B from seizing—Person B will be indifferent as to whether to seize or not in the first place, as the net gain or loss or both options become the same under the current setting. For Person A, he still has to endure a loss of $45 even if Person B pays him a liability payment of $85. His loss will be reduced but not fully compensated.

Scenario #10 shows that the victim still has to suffer, even if justice is on his side. The loophole stems from the limited protection that can be enforced by the justice administrator. A more effective protection would be a liability payment that makes the aggressor worse off, as in Scenario #11, where the administrator inflicts a damage of $150 and exacts a punitive liability payment of $140 from Person B, thereby imposing a total damage of $290 and a net loss of $205 on her and consequentially deterring her from launching aggression in the first place. Person A, in contrast, could pocket a net gain of $10 by appealing to the administrator for help if Person B does pursue aggressions.

The preceding three scenarios demonstrate the significance of whether there is an administrator present or not and the difference that the punitive capability of the administrator can make on whether there is settlement or peace. To deter aggressions from being pursued, we need the administrator to be credible in imposing punitive actions.

Bullying

Besides seizing a good from the other party, Person B may also be able to benefit by bullying Person A, as in Scenario #12 in table 6.5, where Person B offers Person A an option to buy peace for $20. In other words, Person A can keep his Good X if he pays Person B $20. If Person B has to incur a cost of $10 to make that threat credible, she would earn $10 in net terms if Person A complies. It may become worthwhile for both to go with that option, particularly if the administrator is not as punitive as in Scenario

#11. For instance, comparing Scenario #12 with Scenario #10, Person A only needs to bear a smaller loss of $20 (versus $45), while Person B gets $10 instead of getting nothing.

Table 6.5. Peace at a Price?

		Scenario #12
To Person A		
Loss of good if seized		$(100)
Type of defensive maneuver	Buy peace	
Direct cost of maneuver		$(20)
Value of retained Good X		$100
Net benefit/(loss) of maneuver itself		$80
Decision: To buy peace or not?	Yes	
To Person B		
Benefit of seizing		$20
Cost of seizing		
- Logistics cost	$(10)	
- Liability payment payable	-	
Total cost		$(10)
Net benefit/(loss)		$10

We can see that as long as Person A can find a way to make Person B suffer a net loss for being an aggressor, the latter is disincentivized to be so. If neither Person A nor the administrator is able to penalize aggression, it pays for Person B to be an aggressor, which may be by way of directly seizing the good, or bullying. We have the victim either living with his goods being seized or paying for "peace."

Both Being Aggressors

Of course, it could be Person A or the seller who is cheating or takes on the role of aggressor. He may cheat, for instance, by not delivering Good X to Person B after receiving the purchase consideration. Similarly, as spelled out in Scenario #8 in table 6.3, instead of cheating on the consideration, it could also be beneficial for Person A to seize Good Y from Person B, pocketing a gain of $80 and entailing him to a total well-being of $180. In this instance, Person B will suffer a loss of $85, as her Good Y is taken away. The social loss in this case, as in Scenario #7, also equals $5.

Could it be rational for each to seize the other party's possessions? The decision as to whether to deploy resources to seize again depends on whether doing so is expected to elevate oneself to a better state. The benefit obviously lies in the value of the good to be seized from the counterparty.

The cost would be the amount of resources that will be spent on seizing, which may be the sum of investments on building one's own combative capabilities and direct outlays on staging the offensives (or the fee for contracting outside forces for the same purpose), as well as damage that will be suffered if the other party strikes, whether as a response to or in anticipation of one's own offensive moves. Another cost component therefore is the potential loss that may arise if one's endowed good is seized away. The decision, within the cost-and-benefit-analysis framework, is a matter of choosing the highest-yielding proposition among the various possibilities.

Table 6.6. Cost-Benefit Calculus If Both to Seize (Equal Strengths)

	Person A		Person B	
Benefit				
The good seized from the other party	Good Y	$80	Good X	$95
Cost				
Investments on building offensive capabilities	$(20)		$(20)	
Direct outlays on offensives	$(5)	$(25)	$(5)	$(25)
Net benefit/(loss) of seizing		$55		$70
Decision: To seize?		Yes		Yes
Counterparty to strike also				
Damage inflicted by counterparty		$(30)		$(30)
Net benefit/(loss) of seizing, including casualties		$25		$40
Decision: To seize?		Yes		Yes
Own good being seized away as well				
Value of own good being seized	Good X	$(100)	Good Y	$(85)
Net benefit/(loss)		$(75)		$(45)
Decision: To seize?		No		No

As stipulated in table 6.6, we can see that after accounting for the cost of staging the offensives, it is worthwhile for each person to seize the good of the other. However, this is based on two assumptions. The first is that the other party does not strike back. The second is that each is able to keep his or her own good. Without the first, we can see that the gains are trimmed if each is to inflict subsequent damage on the other. For the second one, that obviously cannot be true for both Person A and Person B at the same time. The only possible scenario in this case is that each can seize the other's good, so that each has the other's good only. As a result of that outcome, both will become worse off, with Person A suffering a $75 loss and Person B a $45 loss. The community will be $120 worse off, which is indeed the sum of the resources spent on the offensives ($25 + $25 = $50), the damage inflicted ($30 + $30 = $60), and the fall in total valuation as the two goods change hands (Person A: from $100 to $80 = –$20; Person B: from $85 to $95 = $10; Community: –$20 + $10 = –$10).

We can therefore see that without an all-powerful justice administrator in place, the two players could potentially inflict significant damage on the other, resulting in net loss to all. The question becomes, would that possibility of net loss for all be enough to stop both of them from seizing the good from the other in the first place? Since the shift from net benefit to net loss is premised on the counterparty taking offensive actions as well, that would be the case only if both persons know that the other party is able to inflict significant damage and are convinced that the other will do so if their own good is taken away. That is to say, both will refrain from launching attacks only if both parties believe that doing so always eventually results in they themselves ending up in a worse-off situation.[26] That is to say, a credible renunciation of violence has to be based on the

---

26 As we shall see later in the book, it is in the interests of each party to alter the cost-benefit matrices such that it is costly for others to attack but not so for oneself to do so, in which the relative coercive capacity differences play pivotal roles in determining the outcomes of prosperity or perpetual exploitation. The possible tendency to inflict disproportional damage in case of attack so as to impair the retaliatory capability of the counterparty also plays a part.

conjectures that each one knows that the other party is able and ready to strike back and inflict sufficiently significant damage when being attacked.

STATUS QUO AN OPTION?

The preceding scenario assumes that an individual no longer has the ability to refuse without cost accepting others' propositions that he or she regards as inferior. This implies that the fifth assumption characterizing the neoclassical model is relaxed. The status quo, as a result, is no longer rendered as the worst state or the floor that one could be at when making decisions.

By deducing further from the above, we can see that intentional engagements in loss-making campaigns do not correspond to irrational behavior, or not necessarily so. Such engagements may still be rational moves, even if loss is expected, as long as not doing so is expected to put one in an even worse position (i.e., a bigger negative).

To further comprehend the meaning and importance of the status-quo option, we can first consider the situation typical in the standard neoclassical model, where the status quo is an available option and an individual is given only one alternative proposition to consider. That individual's choice is between taking the alternative proposition and refusing to take it, which typically means staying with the status quo. By taking the alternative proposition, one secures the value or the benefit that is expected to be derived from the pursuit of that proposition, with the cost being the value of sticking to the status quo. In other words, as long as the alternative or pursuing change is expected to bring in a value higher than that of one's existing status, one is expected to take the alternative proposition.

The above highlights the scenario where by not taking the alternative, one could always choose to stay with the initial position or the status quo. That makes the value of the status quo the opportunity cost of pursuing change. However, if the status quo is not an available option, the choice then may not be between the alternative and the existing, or between the new and the old. It may be about adopting the alternative offer or refusing to take it. The value of going for the alternative may be worse than the status quo, but the value of refusing to pick the alternative option may be even worse. That is to say, the choice is about picking the lesser evil.

A simple example would be the choice between handling toxic materials left behind by a bankrupt factory and leaving the materials there and letting the toxic effects spread. Handling them inevitably incurs cost, but doing nothing would possibly be more damaging. The choice here is between two negative propositions.

A further example of a negative status-quo situation is the survival problem. Inaction or ingesting nothing means one will starve to death within days, which for a typical person under normal circumstances is regarded as a negative proposition. To survive, one needs to devise propositions that are expected to bring forth provisional inflows sufficient to meet the outflows or the level of consumptions required to sustain one's life. In a money-denominated and indirect-mode society, these propositions could be expressed as earning money to purchase provisions sufficient for survival.[27]

Depending on whether one likes what one does to earn a living, one may value pursuing those propositions negatively. In this case, the person would hate what he or she does to earn a living. The difference between inaction (not to live) and actions (to live) would be based more on what one values than on what the propositions could earn, that is, the value of living on. Using the rationality postulate, we expect one to endeavor to live as long as the sum of the expected value of one's projected remaining lifespan, if the net cost or "disutility," if applicable, of making a living exceeds the net value of choosing not to live, however discounted and summed. That is to say, if one expects his or her remaining lifespan to be miserably or chronically painful and with no chance of recovery, or regards the option to sacrifice his or her life as substantially valuable, it may become rational for that individual to give up his or her life under the rationality postulate and probably the rationality postulate alone.

---

27 The survival problem could likewise be expressed in nonmonetary terms, like nutrients and gases needed for survival.

As pointed out earlier, the rationality postulate does not necessarily regard the decision to pursue propositions that are expected to bring in negative benefit as irrational, as rationality is concerned only with choosing the option that yields a higher expected benefit. It may be the case that staying put is expected to relegate one to an even worse situation (i.e., a bigger negative). One is therefore expected to pursue the alternative and choose to suffer a lesser pain. In fact, the net expected benefit for the best proposition, even if the options are all negative yielding, is still positive as long as the opportunity cost is a bigger negative proposition.

This helps clarify the meaning of "optimum" or the best possible state. By rationality alone (i.e., without the status-quo option or guarantee), one will choose the best possible option, which could be far worse than one's initial position or the status quo, as the best possible is only the least bad. Nonetheless, that is already sufficient to bring one to the optimum, as the best is chosen at the time of making the decision. Yet this is in stark contrast with the harmonious notion that the optimum carries in the neoclassical model. Choosing the best may not mean making one better than before. The status-quo option is hence crucially important in the ideological connotation of the model.

Other than taking negative propositions, discarding the status-quo option also opens up the strategic possibilities of benefiting oneself by harming others, which is within the rationality domain if such pursuits are expected to put oneself in the best possible position.

MARKET ECONOMY NOT SYNONYMOUS WITH HARMONY

Nonetheless, the essentials of a market economy are still retained. It is the argument that exchanges are always mutually beneficial or detrimental to none that is questionable. Rational self-interest behavior may not necessarily warrant the community to be in harmony; it may only lead us to the second type of accord where antagonisms exist but are not brought out. Nonetheless, integrating those possibilities greatly empowers the explanatory capacity of the model, as cheating and raiding indeed are a fact of life and common tactics in history. They play a significant role in distribution and bargaining issues, and in determining the intensity of competition.

In the following chapters, we will incorporate those possibilities into the analyses to see how to maintain the neoclassical model's tenet within the enlarged rationality domain and to develop a more complete notion of choice and competition.

7

Too Costly to Harm?

In the previous chapter, we relaxed the assumption that the status quo is always an option. As such, an individual may no longer be able to without cost refuse to accept the detrimental propositions of others, in turn making the option of benefiting oneself by harming others available. That may invalidate the neoclassical model's tenet that exchanges are mutually beneficial.

To preserve the model, or the harmonious notion of it, we need to establish that detrimental propositions, though allowed, are always not chosen. For that to be the case under the cost-and-benefit framework, we need to establish that pursuing detrimental propositions is always prohibitively costly. In this chapter, we reformulate the model to see whether and when that is possible.

For that purpose, the neoclassical model's tenet on optima is restated as follows:

> *Pursuing one's own interests will bring each and every individual and consequentially the community as an aggregate to their respective optima that are not worse than the status quo, provided that pursuing propositions to benefit oneself by making others worse off is always prohibitively costly.*

The question becomes, under what circumstances or conditions would those pursuits be prohibitively costly? As discussed in the two scenarios in the previous chapter, aggression is not chosen when

1. There is an all-powerful justice administrator imposing a punitive damage on the aggressor.
2. In the absence of an administrator, both parties are convinced of ending up worse off if they were to strike each other.

Both scenarios are premised on the expectation that the option to strike, as an aggression or a counterstrike, is prohibitively costly and hence not chosen as a result. We will further explore those two scenarios to see if we can pinpoint some common or general conditions. The workings of the administrator are discussed first, particularly regarding whether the administrator, supposedly being just and impartial, would make his or her subjects victims to the administrator's overwhelming might, instead of administering justice for the victims. If so, is it possible to restrain the administrator from doing that? That discussion will bring us to the second scenario, into which the competition process is incorporated. We will then have a framework upon which the neoclassical model is revised and expanded in subsequent chapters to see if it is possible for any party who is contemplating forcing a detrimental proposition onto another always chooses not to do so.

THE FIRST SCENARIO: THE JUSTICE ADMINISTRATOR OR THE BLACK BOX

We first look at the case of relying on a benign and powerful justice administrator or the state to make aggression too costly. The existence of a state has long been assumed in economics,[28] typically taken to be a special entity that is both just and powerful. More specifically related to economics, it is assumed that the state corrects market failures, such as externalities and inadequate provision of public goods. The treatment, however, rests on an implicit assumption that the state is capable of doing that and incentivized to do so—an assumption that we are going to examine further below.

The interest-group and the rent-seeking arguments also challenge the pro-state arguments by pointing out that the behavior of the state is biased

---

28 A. Smith, *The Wealth of Nations* (New York: Bantam Dell, 2003), 874.

by the lobbying activities of interest groups or rent-seeking parties, resulting in favoritism. Yet the focus of those arguments is on the parties influencing the state but not directly on the state itself.

What makes the state "special" or different from other self-interest entities in the community? Why should it be "just" or "impartial"? Dealing with issues *of* public interest does not make the state behave *in* the public's interest. If the state is not impartial, how can we be sure that it will and is able to disallow pursuits of detrimental propositions by any party? Deriving a conclusion that a specific institutional arrangement is good only by assuming that there is an entity or mechanism that makes it good is merely begging the question. After all, if the state is already just and impartial in nature and practice, we may not need to be so concerned about it.[29]

Hence, rather than assuming that the state is intrinsically just and impartial, we assume that it is the same in nature as any other individual in the community: it is a rational self-interest entity. In other words, if it behaves differently, it is because it is being subject to a different cost-and-benefit matrix or incentive mechanism. For instance, if it is on the side of the "victims," that is a result of its cost-and-benefit matrix being structured in such a way that makes it always in its interest to be on the side of the victims. By the same token, it is also possible that its cost-and-benefit matrix warrants it to be an aggressor itself instead of a caretaker of the interests of its subjects.

Characterizing the Black Box: A Self-Interest State

We can summarize the key assumptions of a self-interest justice administrator as follows:

1. **Self-interest rationality:** It cares about its own interests only and pursues the best feasible option as evaluated by the corresponding cost and benefit attributable to itself.

---

29 Indeed, this is similar to Marx's assumption that the repressed proletariats are a different human species that will care about only the collective interests upon assuming absolute power after the collapse or overthrowing via revolutions of the bourgeoisie society (capitalism).

2. **Invincibility:** It is the most powerful party in the community such that any other party that fights against it loses.
3. **Directive to maintain justice:** The justice administrator's assigned directive is to maintain justice, which has the specific meaning that no detrimental propositions are to be pursued toward others, and in the case that any such harm is inflicted on others, the administrator will impose punitive damage on the aggressor.

In case any of the features above clashes with any other, the self-interest rationality prevails.

Invincibility makes the state able to carry out the assigned directive effectively. As it is invincible, any attempt by other parties to confront it fails. As shown in Scenario #11 in table 6.4, by pledging to wield punitive damage on any aggressor and with every party convinced of the administrator's invincibility, as well as its own adherence to the pledge, no party will choose to pursue propositions detrimental to others.

Incentive of Justice

The question then becomes, what kind of incentive structure can ensure that the justice administrator carries out the directive and the directive only? Given the assumption that it is a self-interest party as all other parties in a community are, it is also subject to an incentive system that is typical of any party in a market economy: it charges for use of its services. More specifically, we assume that it charges in accordance with the size of the claims petitioned and, in case of competition for use of its services, sells its services to the highest bidder.

Suppose that Person A, after being cheated by Person B as stipulated in the previous chapter, appeals to the justice administrator to reclaim his loss. Since Person A is a victim, the administrator is obligated, according to the directive, to reclaim the loss for him. Further, suppose that Person A will pay the administrator in proportion to the size of the reclaim obtained. The directive and the incentive look compatible.

However, given that the administrator is a self-interest entity, it will take on any option that is rendered the most beneficial to itself. If compliance with the directive does not bring in a benefit, pecuniary or not, that surpasses the benefit that may be offered by a party lobbying for noncompliance (or noncompliance itself does not constitute a cost that offsets the benefit being offered for noncompliance), the incentive structure then becomes incompatible with the directive. As specified, since the administrator, as a self-interest player, will work for whoever pays it a higher fee (where the self-interest rationality postulate takes precedence), Person B can fend off Person A's reclaim efforts simply by paying the administrator a higher fee. The directive or the obligation to save the victims loses its relevance immediately.

A bidding process may result if both persons try to offer the administrator a higher fee. Since Person A is commissioning the administrator to make Person B pay for the amount being cheated, the maximum fee that he or she is willing to pay for the claim service is the size of the cheat. Yet since the cheat is also the very amount that Person B intends to commission the administrator to save her from paying, the maximum amount that Person B is willing to pay the administrator is also the size of the cheat. The bidding process would, therefore, result in offers of the same amount being made, which is the size of the cheat. However, if the administrator is allowed to and does threaten to inflict punitive damage on Person B, the latter may be willing to pay a fee higher than the amount cheated, pushing her to place a bid that trumps that of Person A. Under such a setting, rather than reclaiming losses for the victims, the administrator protects the interests of the aggressor because of the punitive-damage clause.

We can see that if the administrator is to work for any party that pays better, there is no guarantee that its behavior is compatible with what enforcing the directive requires.[30] Without an effective incentive or restraint mechanism in place, a mere directive could hardly discipline the administrator.

---

30 This requires the victim to always offer the administrator better terms.

Since any gains that could be made from cheating would eventually be in the hands of the administrator, no matter who wins the bid, it is the administrator that stands to be the true winner. Moreover, given its superior coercive capability, all attempts by its subjects to fend off its aggression or to reclaim their losses are bound to fail. Such an incentive structure just makes it all too favorable for the administrator to be the biggest aggressor and vice-doer instead of being an impartial agent of justice. The administrator is best positioned to extract maximum gains from the subjects.

Confronting Justice

As long as we have a self-interest justice administrator in place, appending a directive to it will not be sufficient to make it just and impartial. With no directive, this leads us to anarchy, through which there is no just and fair justice administrator but an all-powerful player in the community. All participants are the same in nature, even though not necessarily in size or power. Players are free to strike, and if combative or confrontational tactics are deployed, whether through personal efforts or by employing services of others, they are all at a cost. The question becomes whether it is possible, under such an anarchical setting, to have the administrator or the overpowering aggressor restrained.

As discussed in chapter 6, other than the scenario of relying on the overwhelmingly mighty administrator, there is another scenario where detrimental propositions are not pursued, which is where both Person A and Person B renounce aggression based on the belief that the other, once attacked, will strike back for significant damage. Applying that to the current setting suggests that the administrator could be checked if there is another party capable of inflicting prohibitively costly damage on it. However, since by the invincibility assumption the justice administrator is already assumed to be the most powerful in the community, any other party that engages it loses.

An alternative would be via the collusion of the subjects. The collusion could take a noninstitutionalized form of revolt or revolution, or it could also be attained via some institutional mechanism facilitating collusion so that the colluded efforts could penalize the aggressor or even dislodge it from the capacity altogether. For that to happen, the community members need to be incentivized to organize themselves to form alternatives to compete for the administrator position so as to impose a credible disciplinary force on whichever party is in the administrator capacity.

The formation of an effective counterforce could likewise be aided by vesting less power with the capacity, particularly discretionary power,[31] such that the disparity between the administrator and the subjects is smaller, or by unbundling the power to different layers of administration in order to institute checks and balances among the parties. Obviously, subjecting the incumbent to more frequent dislodging threats could also increase the power of the disciplinary force.

Exposing the administrator to disciplinary forces, as depicted above, is in effect subjecting it to competition for the administrator capacity. Being displaced from the position means loss of further benefits that could be earned from the role and possibly liability for previous excesses. If the colluded efforts could deliver a sufficient threat of counterstrike, the administrator may be deterred from pursuing detrimental propositions on its subjects, resembling the second scenario where both parties refrain from launching aggression to avoid being struck back. However, if no alternative faction that is capable of competing against or replacing the aggressor can be formed, any disciplinary mechanism, institutionalized or not, would hardly be strong enough to impose the hoped-for restraining effect in practice. In fact, no matter which type of mechanism one is in, as long as it fails to generate effective competition, the community is prone to being locked in a social structure where the poor and vulnerable are captivated and capitalized by the strong. That is to say, the intensity of competition plays a major role in determining whether the disciplinary mechanism is effective and hence whether detrimental propositions will be pursued, as is further discussed below.

---

31 To the limit, this would mean that the administrator is given only well-defined execution power, which is more toward the arrangements under a representative democracy if not also the ideal stipulated by the direct democracy thesis (e.g., referendums and vetoes) as well.

THE SECOND SCENARIO: COMPETITION DYNAMICS

The Bidding Process and the Availability of the Better

The neoclassical model typically uses the bidding process to illustrate the dynamics of competition. For instance, under competition, a worker will find a job that pays him or her a wage rate that equals his or her contribution to the exchange value of the goods or services he or she helps to make or provide. Suppose that the worker's contribution accounts for half of the value of the finished item, which his or her employer sells at $10 apiece in the market. That means his or her labor service is worth $5 apiece. If he or she is paid only $3, his or her employer will pocket a net gain of $2 apiece by employing him or her.

That gain, however, may induce an alternative employer to come and offer the worker, say, $4 apiece for his or her service. Assuming that all other costs are the same for the employers, the new employer could still pocket an extra net gain of $1 apiece by employing him or her. However, there may yet be another employer willing to pay a wage rate that is higher than the $4 rate to get the smaller but still positive extra net gain. One would expect the bidding process to continue until the wage rate reaches the breakeven level of $5 apiece where no more extra gain could be made.

Can the wage rate be higher than $5 apiece? As an employer will suffer a loss at any wage rate that is above that level, the worker will find no employer willing to employ his or her labor service at those rates, provided information cost is negligible. To gain employment, he or she needs to revise his or her wage demand down to where an employer is not expected to bear a loss by employing him or her, which is not to be higher than $5 apiece in the current example.

Taking the two strands together, the bidding or the competition for the worker's service among prospective employers drives and limits the wage rate to the level of what the worker's labor service is worth in the market (i.e., $5 apiece). If outside bidders know the current and the maximum prices to be offered by the incumbent buyer, they will come only if they know they can outbid the incumbent and do so at a gain. On the same rationale, incumbent employers, being aware of the possibility that an outsider will come if a gain to the latter is credible, will raise the wage rate if their aggregate cost levels are the same and they are selling the same product, giving no one an edge in the bidding.

The situation where all pay the same wage rate and sell their finished products at the same price in fact resembles the perfect competition setting in economics, which hinges on all selling the same product and having the same cost level. However, if the incumbent is disadvantaged in one way or another, warranting him or her to lose in the bidding, he or she may quit the business. In contrast, if there is one producer who is able to generate a higher value from his or her workers, other potential bidders and sellers will be outcompeted by that highest-value user.

However, how much would the highest-value bidder pay the worker? If the worker is paid at the maximum (or the share of the worker's contribution in the market value of the finished product), the employer pockets no extra profit by employing that worker. That incentivizes the employer to stop short of paying the worker to the maximum unless being forced to do so. In fact, he or she only needs to pay a wage rate slightly higher than the maximum that the second-highest-value user is willing to pay, as that is enough to deter all others from coming to compete against him or her.

So how much the wage rate could be bid up depends on the effective supply of better offers. When there is no better offer, the bidding stops. That may happen even before the wage rate reaches the maximum rate that the employer is willing to pay, which as mentioned is the breakeven level for the employer or the share of the worker's contribution in the market value of the finished product. It is the ceiling rate but may not be offered at all.

For that to happen, that employer needs to be the only one in the market who is able to derive the highest and the higher value (in terms of the share of the workers' contribution in the market value of the finished product) from the worker's service. That is the incentive for the employer or firm to improve itself to become and remain the best.

Nonetheless, although a worker may not get the maximum an employer is willing to pay, the more offers there are, the more likely the worker gets better terms. The same is true for biddings for any other goods or services. Getting back to Person A in our earlier example, if other parties could go to him to bid for his Good X, where he is in effect competing against Person B, the chance that Person A gets a better deal will be higher. Competition dynamics as such could release an individual from being confined to the limited bids made by the incumbent employer or buyer and give the seller other bids to choose from. Competition among interested buyers is likely to compel all buyers to improve their bids, benefiting counterparties like the worker and Person A.

In fact, the force to improve bids could bring forth other benefits to the sellers. For instance, propositions that are outright detrimental to others would be off the table. Cheating attempts may also be squeezed out as interested buyers, when competing for Person A's Good X, may make their bids more solid by severing all possible strings or loopholes for cheating. The more choices there are, the more likely it is that one can be free from the constrictions of detrimental propositions imposed by counterparties. The dislodgement or disengagement threat indeed resonates with the earlier scenario, where the threat to be displaced is able to keep an aggressor from pursuing propositions that are detrimental to the interests of the others.

In sum, competition dynamics puts a good or service in the hands of those users who value them most. Prices, however, may not gyrate to the best values they can command in the market. The effective functioning of the bidding process and the robustness of the neoclassical model depend on whether there are better bids or offers for the subject under consideration (e.g., the worker's labor service or Good X of Person A). The more choices there are—or the more intense the competition is—the more likely the terms will improve and the more likely the propositions intended to benefit by cheating or harming are forced out. The availability of the better alternatives is the prime dynamic driving competition.

Competition Beneficial to Everyone?

The above is where the neoclassical model stops. However, what would the incumbent employer think about the onset of competition? In fact, he or she is made worse off by the competition or the incoming employers.

The $2-apiece net gain originally retained by that employer is transferred to the worker or the new employer as a result of the competition. This redistribution has benefited the worker or the new employer at his or her expense. In other words, not every party will be happy with the outcomes. Even if all trades are made with the same contracting parties, one or more parties are still bound to lose from the onset of new competition, with the incumbent employer, whose gain would have been bigger if there was no competition, being the most probable victim.

Within the context of cost-and-benefit analysis, every individual will pursue the propositions best for himself or herself. He or she will not stand idle and accept the smaller gain when competition comes. The incumbent will evaluate the feasible options for his or her interests. As in our previous example, the incumbent employer may become willing to expend a maximum of $2 apiece to stop any bidding for the labor service. He or she may raise the cost for his or her competitors to make deals with the workers. That could be achieved by, say, lobbying the government to enact a tariff or other protective measures against such moves (e.g., licensing or regulatory requirements against foreign companies looking to commence local operations). Or he or she may prevent the workers from dealing with the potential bidders. The workers may be locked up physically or contractually: they may be kept at the employer's factories or quarters, or punitive clauses might be added to the employment contracts (e.g., forfeiture of bonus or pension accumulated for "early" contract termination).

Whatever the means being deployed, as long as the incumbent succeeds in reclaiming his or her loss or making defections more costly, the gain for the worker or the prospective entrant will be trimmed, if not eliminated totally. This will consequentially disincentivize prospective competitors to bid for the worker's service and undermine the intensity of competition.

ASYMMETRIC PREFERENCE OF COMPETITION INTENSITY

Does it follow, however, that the employer prefers repressing competition under every circumstance? To avoid being captivated by the worker, the incumbent employer may also want to have access to similarly capable workers who are competing among themselves for his or her wage bids. The more workers who are available, the more likely it is that there is a worker willing to work at a wage rate lower than the prevailing level, and the more likely also that the wage rate is being pulled down. We can see that similar to a worker wanting access to alternative employers, it would be in an employer's interests to have access to alternative workers or intense competition among the workers.

This is, of course, applicable not only to a buyer of labor service but of any good—who would prefer dealing with a pool of sellers competing among themselves for his or her patronage. A buyer would purchase a good provided that the price he or she pays for is within his or her affordability and is not higher than his or her valuation of the good, and more importantly, there is no better alternative. To court the buyer's business, sellers may lower their prices or make their offers more enticing by other nonprice means. Expectedly, one seller improving an offer may well compel others to follow suit. That may continue until the price reaches the breakeven point or the cost of that good.[32] With more sellers around, the chance for a buyer to obtain a better deal is higher.

Similarly, a seller, like the worker who is selling his or her labor service, would prefer there to be a lot of buyers competing for the goods or services that he or she is offering. The more bids around, the more likely that the seller is to get a better deal. However, just as competition among buyers will drive up the purchase price, the size of gain available to the final buyers will be smaller as well. This implies that it is unlikely that buyers, if given a choice, would prefer having more intense competition among themselves. By the same token, sellers will also not prefer increasingly fierce competition against one another, as this will benefit buyers at their own expense.

---

32 Selling at prices below that cost level means the sellers will suffer a loss. They may refrain from selling in order to wait for prices to go higher if they believe low prices are only transient, or they may quit the business if they believe that the loss-making prices will last.

In short, a seller would prefer competition among buyers on the one hand and the absence of such among sellers, actual or potential, on the other hand. A buyer, in contrast, wants to have intense competition among the sellers for his or her patronage and no other buyers bidding on the goods or services he or she is interested in.[33] That is to say, each individual has an asymmetric preference of competition intensity: no competition on his or her side but intense competition on the counterparty's side.

Obviously, the asymmetric preferences of the individuals when aggregated together are bound to be incompatible. The worker naturally prefers there being only himself or herself in the labor market but with a lot of prospective employers competing for his or her service. That clashes directly against the preferences of the employers, who all prefer having access to numerous workers but only one employer in the market. Yet the second preference strand of the employers puts them in conflict mode against one another.

What would be the result? In view of the potential gain, all are willing to apportion a certain amount of resources to put themselves in a more advantageous position (e.g., by differentiating themselves from others by being more specialized, in effect reducing the size of competition, or by selling their products in new markets, thereby having access to more buyers), or to augment the competition landscape to the same effect (e.g., forbidding competitors from directly contacting those on one's payroll, such as the UEFA rule that forbids football clubs looking for new players to get on board to bypass a player's incumbent club for direct negotiation if that player is not free).

The forces to fence off and to foster competition coexist and battle against each other. Different markets at different times may have different resultant intensities of competition. Moreover, coexistence of the

---

33 A seller may fight hard to establish access to other markets, even if success in such may expose him or her to more competition from other sellers. This does not suggest that the seller prefers competition against other sellers. What the seller wants is to have access to a larger pool of buyers, with competition with other sellers only a necessary evil that is not expected to constitute a loss that outweighs the benefit of having the fought-for access to more buyers.

conflicting forces is not unique to the market mechanism and can indeed be found in other, if not all, economic, political, social, and interpersonal structures as well.[34] For instance, while many under a repressive regime struggle hard to break the grip, there are also others who endeavor to become part of the establishment and to sustain the regime. Similarly, while some dictators may continue to maintain the squeeze on their subjects who may already be very impoverished, others may choose to loosen the control gradually and still others may lose the power and see their rule collapsed.

* * *

We can see that a powerful state can forestall or preempt aggressions or the pursuits of detrimental propositions among subjects, but there is no intrinsic mechanism to restrain that state from becoming the biggest aggressor. In fact, the state is the best positioned to be so. Echoing the scenario where two parties are able to inflict prohibitively costly revenges when attacked such that detrimental propositions are not pursued, the power of the state may be held in check by means of an effective disciplinary mechanism that acts as a virtual counterforce to contain or eliminate excesses. Intense competition, which depends on the availability of better alternatives, could be such a disciplinary force when structured appropriately.

Competition intensity in the neoclassical model is a given fixity rather than a choice variable. However, it is unreasonable to assume that an individual, enticed by the potentially larger gains from, say, being a monopoly, does not contemplate putting himself or herself in such a more lucrative position, and those who would be harmed as a result to do nothing to counter that from happening. Instead of a given fixity, the intensity of competition shall be the product of the battles among conflicting competition-intensity preferences of the parties involved.

---

34 Perhaps unless we are in a community—large or small, complex or simple, impersonal or intimate—where competition is no longer necessary or the members of the community all have their mind-sets evolved into a state where competition has become an obsolete concept, these conflicting forces will remain an integral part of any type of community.

It has also become possible to have a certain level of competition intensity that would be sufficient to hold the incumbent or the strongest in check or to make the pursuits of detrimental propositions too costly. In the following chapters, we will revise the neoclassical model in that light by expanding on the competition-intensity preference within the cost-benefit-analysis framework in order to further analyze those possibilities and delineate the associated conditions correspondingly.

8

Preference of Competition Intensity

THE IMPORTANCE OF COMPETITION INTENSITY

The neoclassical tenet that all exchanges are mutually beneficial hinges on the component that no propositions detrimental to others are pursued. Yet pursuits of those propositions may be perfectly rational. For the tenet to remain valid within the enlarged domain, we are going to look for conditions that make pursuing those detrimental propositions, while permissible, always not chosen. Under the cost-benefit-analysis framework, this implies that propositions are always prohibitively costly to be pursued.

Two arguments may confine one's choices as such. The first, as spelled out in earlier chapters, assumes the presence of a justice administrator that is combatively most powerful and also will inflict reciprocal damage on any other party that has pursued propositions detrimental to others. Due to its unrivaled combat capability, merely pledging to inflict punitive damage is sufficient to put up a formidable deterrent against any party to pursue aggressions. But that very invincibility also gives the administrator the de facto monopoly in vice-doing and may even open up the possibility of other parties buying from it the license to harm.[35] In other words, while it is true that the assumed presence of such an administrator could make detrimental pursuits prohibitively costly, disciplining the administrator itself poses a greater problem and may result in a repressive totalitarian regime.

---

35 The dominant may keep its rule sustained by selling the "licenses" and specializing in being the strongest coercively.

To examine if it is possible to discipline the administrator within the rationality postulate, the assumption that it is "just" (which is a handier way to assume the problem away than an approximation of reality) needs to be abandoned. That is, we are assuming that the administrator is of the same in nature as any other party in the community, in that it pursues its self-interest subject to the incentive structure applicable to it. Differences in behavior, if any, should be due to it facing a different incentive structure, but not the assumption that it is intrinsically different or assigned a directive to maintain justice.

That brings us back to the fundamental issue: how is an individual incentivized and, at the same time, disciplined? Since under the rationality postulate an individual always chooses the propositions he or she expects to be the most beneficial, the more intense competition becomes (meaning the more alternatives available), the less likely it is for him or her to be restricted to a choice of wholly negative propositions and the more significant the dislodgment threat would be on the incumbent aggressor.

However, in the neoclassical model, competition intensity is an exogenously given parameter and cannot be altered by any participant, no matter which market structure one is in. One simply cannot change the competition landscape but has to live with it. Whether an individual finds himself or herself as the monopoly of all energy sources on the planet or as a grocery store owner suddenly facing the onslaughts of supermarket chains is wholly a matter of fate. The neoclassical model is concerned only with what happens under each of the specified market-structure settings, which are perfect competition, monopolistic competition, oligopoly, and monopoly. The model does not set itself the tasks of analyzing the different settings in an integrated coherent framework and determining whether there are any dynamics working to alter the competition intensity as stipulated in each of the market-structure settings. The different market structures, representing the four bands of competition intensity, are assumed to be discrete and not linked.

Yet as argued in the previous chapter, one is not only incentivized to foster competition to one's benefit but also to restrain it when it works against oneself. The rivalries among the colonial empires or among new-comers and giants for a leading role in industries like communications and media have all illustrated that competition intensity is an important organic strategic-decision variable rather than a given fixity.

In other words, a market may not become intensely competitive by itself. A market that is already intensely competitive also may not remain so indefinitely. Putting the two together, we can see that an intensely competitive market results when it is too costly for everyone to restrain competition but it is beneficial to foster it, such that competition intensity is maximized and the chance of detrimental propositions being pursued minimized—in turn, giving the neoclassical tenet that all exchanges are mutually beneficial the best chance of being materialized.

PREFERENCE OF COMPETITION INTENSITY: AN ILLUSTRATION

To further analyze one's choice on competition intensity, we are going to develop a model using a stylized medieval castle town as an illustration. There are three parties in this fictional town: Dominants, Subordinates, and Outsiders. The Dominant is assumed to be well endowed and owns the castle town, including the farmlands upon which the Subordinate works. He may also build castle walls to surround the town to defend it against foreign threats and maintain an army to extend his interests by besieging or conquering neighboring castles. As for the Outsider, he may be a merchant coming to the castle town for trade, a raider to seize goods away, or even an aggressor trying to replace the incumbent and become the new Dominant.

Here, there could be a number of possible types of relationship between the Dominant and the Subordinate. The Subordinate may be a slave who works in accordance with what the Dominant wills in exchange for food and shelter, or a freeman, which is more like a tenant paying the Dominant a rent that is fixed or varies with, say, the size of the harvest and is allowed to keep or sell the residual. Of course there could be other relationship types between the two, but no matter which type of relationship they are in, they are essentially trading the same items: labor service of the Subordinate and the right to farm on the lands of the Dominant. The consideration may be in the form of produce, shelter, the prevailing medium of exchange adopted, or any combination of those.

For the present purpose, it is assumed that the Subordinate pays the Dominant a rental that is fixed and is in the form of produce, in exchange for the rights to farm and live on the Dominant's land, as well as to keep, consume, or sell the residual. From the Dominant's perspective, he buys the labor service of the Subordinate for making of the produce, to be delivered to him in the name of rental, by means of the right to farm and live on his lands as well as allowing the Subordinate to keep or sell any residual produce.

The Dominant as a Buyer

Instead of the rental aspect, the focus here is on the residual that the Subordinate is allowed to keep and put up for sale in the markets, where the Dominant may be one of the potential buyers. Obviously, as a buyer of the produce, the objective of the Dominant is to minimize the purchase consideration for the Subordinate's produce put up for sale. To do that, his preference of competition intensity is to restrain competition on his or the buyer's side so as to limit the Subordinate's choice in selling the produce on the one hand,[36] and to foster competition on the seller's side to expand his own choice of supply on the other hand. Although the preferred competition intensities in the two markets differ, they share the same objective, which is to undermine the Subordinate's ability to get a higher consideration for the produce, particularly from him.

As specified, the Dominant is in command of some coercive capability. It may be deployed to attain the first strategy strand of restricting the Subordinate's access to buyers by, for instance, curtailing the traveling freedom of the Subordinate, or fencing him from the outside markets.

---

36 Since the Dominant is also the landlord, he could achieve the same by raising the quantity of produce to be paid as rent.

Since the Subordinate can retain the produce for own consumption (i.e., sell to himself), that means he would sell the residual to others only if doing so brings in proceeds higher than the value of his consuming the produce himself. Without any access to other buyers, the Subordinate can only choose between selling the produce to the Dominant or to himself.

Under the circumstances, based on the availability of the better alternative argument discussed in the previous chapter, to acquire the produce the Dominant only needs to offer a consideration slightly better than the value that the Subordinate could derive from consuming the produce himself. Unless there would be no trade anyway had there been no fencing, the opportunity to sell at a higher price to the Outsider is concealed as a consequence of the fencing. The consideration for the produce is squeezed, benefiting the Dominant as the buyer. The buildup of the capability to fence therefore constitutes a strategic move by the Dominant to restrain competition to his benefit but at the Subordinate's expense.

Other than blocking the Subordinate from forming ties with the Outsider, the Dominant may adopt other strategies to minimize the purchase consideration. Since the Subordinate owns no land and, by assumption, is unable to migrate to another castle, if he does not buy the right to work on the Dominant's land, he may starve to death. The Dominant may therefore only need to pay the Subordinate a subsistence level of consideration to secure the produce as, for the Subordinate, that is still better than his next best option, which is starvation.[37]

---

37 As a further example, suppose that the Subordinate has agreed to pay $70 worth of the produce to the Dominant as rental every year, and suppose the Subordinate needs $30 worth of the produce for subsistence. If the harvest turns out to be only $90 in a certain year, leaving the Subordinate with only $20 after the rental payment, he would not have enough for subsistence. To the Dominant, taking in $10 less still gives him $60 worth of the produce as rental. If the Dominant renders the Subordinate to be "worth keeping alive," he may be willing to accept a rental payment of $10 less for the current year, which may be assigned as debt to be repaid at a later date when the harvests are good. The Subordinate would become indebted, and the Dominant would have a $10 advantage carried over to the next period to slice away any additional produce from the Subordinate in case of a good harvest. To the same effect, by manipulating the size of the rental, the Dominant may be able to lock the Subordinate into the choice between subsistence and starvation.

The ability to relegate the Subordinate to such a subsistence choice does not have to come from ownership of the land. Suppose, instead of the Dominant, it is the Subordinate who owns the farmlands. The Dominant, however, is still in command of the coercion force. Under such a setting, the Dominant may only need to threaten the Subordinate with choosing to either have all his goods seized away or keep a quantity of the produce that is sufficient only for subsistence and yield the rest to him. As a further alternative, the Dominant may threaten not to protect the Subordinate in the event of raids or invasions. The Subordinate may hence prefer buying off those threats by paying the Dominant a "protection" or "security maintenance" fee—of a size that effectively forces the Subordinate to choose between starvation and subsistence.

Counterthreat

Indeed, fencing, land ownership, and the command of a coercion force serve the same purpose in the above setting, which is to limit the choice of the Subordinate such that the Subordinate's incentive calculus is biased toward giving more of the produce to the Dominant and for the lowest possible consideration. However, what if the Subordinate threatens the Dominant that without his contribution, the lands would stay idle and no harvests would be made, such that not only the Subordinate but also the Dominant would starve?

Assuming that the Subordinate's threat is feasible, the credibility of that threat hinges on the cost for the Dominant to find a substitute supply of produce. The substitute could be another Subordinate, produce that could be acquired from other sources, or produce piled up at his storehouses. To the Dominant, the gain from employing the Subordinate is the sum of the value of the produce the latter submits to him, the value of any other services that may be tendered to him, and the net gain from any of the residual the Subordinate sells to him. If there is a substitute that brings a higher gain to the Dominant after accounting for the threat posed by the Subordinate, then the Dominant may no longer find it worthwhile to keep the Subordinate but will get the substitute to work for him instead, in turn dismissing the threat.

That is to say, for the Dominant to agree to the Subordinate's demand for a cut in the amount to be submitted, the resulting level has to remain higher than what may be offered by the next best substitute available to the Dominant. That gives the Subordinate a leeway in the amount of the difference between his offer and the level of the offer made by the next best substitute.[38]

From Paying Rental to Receiving Wages

Now suppose that the economic relationship between the Dominant and the Subordinate is such that the Dominant gets all the produce and pays a fixed quantity of the produce as wages to the Subordinate instead of the Subordinate paying rent to the Dominant, and that the Subordinate is demanding a higher wage from the Dominant. As illustrated by the example below, the dynamic is indeed very similar to that in the previous case.

Assume that the value of total outputs per period submitted by the Subordinate is worth $10 to the Dominant, as shown in all the scenarios in table 8.1. In Scenario A, the Subordinate is given $5 worth of resources as his wage in effect. The Dominant thereby gains $5 ($10 – $5) by employing the Subordinate. Suppose that the substitute supply asks for a wage of $6, which is higher than that of the Subordinate by $1. However, as in Scenario B, if the Subordinate demands a raise of $2, meaning that keeping him only gives the Dominant a net gain of $3, the Dominant will abandon him and take in the substitute supply instead, as the latter gives him a net gain of $4, which has become a better option.

---

38   The same calculus could also be used to illustrate the case of the Subordinate having all his produce seized away by the Dominant, resulting in the Subordinate starving to death. If the cost of seizing is negligible, the Dominant gains via the value of the whole lot of the produce. Yet without the Subordinate, the Dominant has to find some replacement supply to meet his needs. In other words, the cost to the Dominant of letting the Subordinate die would be the cost of finding the replacement supply (say, in the form of lower rental payments) in subsequent periods, which could be significantly higher, especially if the vice of the Dominant is known to the prospective substitutes.

Table 8.1. Challenges

	Scenarios		
	A	**B**	**C**
Value of total outputs produced by the Subordinate	10	10	10
Consideration payable to the Subordinate	5	7	11
Cost of substitute capable of producing the same	6	6	11
Decision	Keep the Subordinate	Employ the substitute	Disengage

Could the Subordinate raise his wage rate above the value the Dominant attaches to his outputs, as in Scenario C? As doing so would render the Dominant in a worse-off position no matter which worker he takes, he would choose not to employ either the Subordinate or the substitute who are demanding the same loss-creating wage rate. The Dominant would instead consider the cost of producing the outputs himself. If that still puts him in a position worse than not producing at all, he may quit making those outputs altogether so as to avoid suffering the loss.

To avoid being trumped as such, the Dominant will therefore consider the benefit and cost of fostering competition in the produce supply market. For instance, he may maintain dependable links with other sources. He may stack up stocks as contingent measures. He might also keep a pool of subordinates working for him so that any shortfalls caused by the defection of a few could be made up by others more readily. In short, the key to successful mitigation of the threat involves maintaining a credible availability of alternative and competing supply, constituting the second strand of his preference of competition intensity as a buyer.

When the Dominant is a buyer, whether as a landlord or an employer, it is in his interests to minimize the bargaining strength of his counterparty, or the Subordinate in the current example. To do that, he prefers having ineffectual competition on the buyer's side (e.g., by fencing off the Subordinate from the Outsider) and intense competition on the counterparty or the seller's side (e.g., by gathering a pool of suppliers fiercely competing among themselves), making his preference of competition intensity asymmetric. With a dependent and expendable Subordinate, the

Dominant is well positioned to buy the produce (or the labor services of the Subordinate) at minimal prices and maintain his dominance.

As a Seller

With the produce on hand or secured, what is the Dominant going to do with it? He may take it up for consumption by him or his estate, keep it as contingent reserves against events like challenges by the Subordinate or bad weather, or sell it to the Outsider.

A look at his valuation schedule, as shown in table 8.2, gives a better picture of this.

Table 8.2. Valuation Schedule of the Dominant

Unit of produce	Value if for consumption	Value if for reserves	Decided purpose	Final value given the chosen purpose
1st	$30	$11	Consumption	$30
2nd	$25	$9	Consumption	$25
3rd	$20	$7	Consumption	$20
4th	$15	$5	Consumption	$15
5th	$10	$3	Reserves	$11
6th	$5	$1	Consumption	$10
7th	$0	$1	Reserves	$9
8th	$0	$1	Reserves	$7
9th	$0	$1	Indifferent	$5
10th	$0	$1	Indifferent	$5
	$105	$40		$137

Suppose the produce is divided into ten units. For consumption, the Dominant values the first unit of produce at $30 and $5 less for each of the successive units. As shown in the corresponding column, he attaches a zero value from the seventh unit onward. If it is to be piled up as reserves, the Dominant values the first unit at $11, with each successive unit dropping $2 in value until reaching a stable value of $1 from the sixth unit onward.

To decide whether each unit is for consumption or reserves, we just need to compare the applicable value of each unit when deployed for the corresponding purpose. The first four units all command a higher valuation if being used for consumption than if stored as reserves. The fifth unit, however, entails a higher value when stored ($11) than consumed ($10) and hence will be stacked up accordingly. Similarly, the sixth unit will be for consumption, while the seventh and the eighth units are taken as reserves. As for the remaining two units, which give the same values for either purpose, one will be for consumption and the other for storage.

From the final value column (which gives the value of each unit of the good on the corresponding chosen purpose), we can work out the Dominant's supply schedule simply by taking the values in that column in reverse, as that gives the schedule of the minimum value of each unit of the produce that the seller demands in order for him to sell that unit. For instance, to give up one unit of his ten in possession (i.e., his last unit), a compensation of at least the value that unit is worth to him, or $5, is required. On that information, if the Outsider values that unit higher than $5, he is incentivized to come to bid for that unit from the Dominant. This also suggests that if the Dominant is the highest-value user in the buyer market for all and every unit of the produce, no other buyer is willing to come to bid for that produce.

However, if the Dominant is not the highest-value user but the other potential buyers know that they will be outbid by the highest-value user among them, would the outcome be that only the highest bidder comes? If that is the case, the highest bidder, aware that the other buyers are not coming to compete against him, may in turn refrain from bidding at a price higher than the rest but only at a level that is merely slightly better than what is asked by the Dominant. To keep that from happening, it may be in the Dominant's interests to keep the access open for other prospective buyers so that they can make replacement bids readily if the highest-value user bids as such.

There are other advantages for the Dominant to maintain an open buyer market for his produce. As the value attached to each successive unit by any individual tends to fall, the corresponding bid price that each buyer is willing to make also tends to fall after each successful bid. Unless the valuation schedules of the individuals differ materially, the price placed by an individual bidding for his second unit is likely to be lower than that by another individual bidding the same as his first unit. That means that in order to keep the bidding prices at high levels, the seller would make the market access open to all prospective buyers such that, for instance, when the second unit is up for bidding, the bid price placed by the second-highest bidder (who is only bidding for his first unit) is likely to be higher than that placed by the successful bidder of the first unit (who is now bidding for his second unit), which is likely to be valued as inferior to his first. It is therefore in the Dominant's interests to foster and maintain intense competition in the counterparty market or the demand side when he himself is a seller so as to keep the bids high.

Moreover, to win a bid, as argued, the bidder needs to pay a price that is higher than the value the seller attaches to that unit of produce and the highest bidding price offered by the other buyers, whichever is highest. If the bidders collude, the bidding prices may just be slightly higher than the value the seller attaches to each unit of the produce. It is therefore preferable for the Dominant for the competition among the buyers to be as intense as possible to lessen the chance of their colluding.

For the other strand of his competition preference as a seller, the Dominant is interested in fencing off other sellers from the buyers to prevent them from being wooed away. Other than physically confining the buyers to a place (like an auction or the only store in town), the Dominant may buy all the surplus produce from the sellers first or acquire the sellers.

In short, the asymmetric preference of the Dominant, as a seller of the produce, is to face no competition pressure from other sellers but to have intense competition among the prospective buyers. That is, as a buyer he prefers intense competition on the counterparty side and ineffectual competition on his own. That asymmetric preference pattern, however, only covers the value or the benefit side of those strategies. The following chapter will deal with the cost side.

9

Value and Cost

The previous chapter discusses preferences on competition intensity. Since putting one's asymmetric preferences in place requires investing resources that could be deployed for other purposes, a rational individual will fence off or foster competition only if doing so is expected to bring in the highest gain (or the least loss) among the available options.

Evidently, the expected benefit of each endeavor is the change in the favorable direction of, as applicable, the purchase or the sale consideration. To do so by, for instance, fencing off competitors, the Dominant may acquire land and build castles, probably reinforced by garrisons. If his intent is to foster competition, he may build roads or ports, set up marketplaces and organize regular exchanges, or even provide financing to facilitate trades.

Such maneuvers require putting in resources that could be used elsewhere, suggesting the need to integrate cost into the decision calculus. Doing so, however, may lead to a strategy that is different from considering the competition-intensity preference alone. As a buyer of the produce from the Subordinate, due to the high costs, the Dominant may no longer find it beneficial to dampen competition from other buyers (by cutting off the links between the Subordinate and the Outsider, for instance) or foster competition among the sellers by maintaining a pool of competing produce suppliers. Likewise, when evaluating as a seller, the Dominant may compare the net expected gains of the various options of selling the produce, such as selling to other buyers, the Outsider only, or none at all (i.e., keeping the produce for himself), and he may not find the option of open-ing to all, which is expected to result in the highest competition intensity among the buyers, the highest-yielding one. He may also determine that, say, making himself the monopoly seller in the locality by preventing other sellers from reaching his buyers does not bring in a net expected benefit higher than that from letting them trade unrestrictedly. The significance of cost as a factor in the value matrix is shown in the discussion on the realization of value below.

BASIS FOR IMPROVEMENT: VALUATION DIFFERENCE AND THE SEARCH FOR THE HIGHEST VALUE

Nature has endowed us with an essentially fixed amount of physical re-sources, yet they may be repackaged or recombined in different manners. Whether the sizes or the patterns of the organic growth therefrom are altered or not, valuations may change accordingly. An abandoned elder-ly cow, after years of services on the farm, commands a valuation quite different from a meticulously reared cow purposed for sale as top-grade steak at high-end restaurants. Trees cut for making chopsticks, furniture, or houses versus those preserved as the habitat for rare species also give rise to very divergent valuations, especially between businesspeople and ecologists. Chemical elements and compounds found readily in the nature combined in a different way may release the energy imbued more effec-tively and hence command drastically different valuations. When a good is exchanged, the proceeds are aligned not only with the resources embed-ded but also with the ideas as to how the resources are bundled to create that good, and it is the ideas or the ability to repackage or recombine the resources in ways that command higher valuations that can be even more valuable.

With the ability to combine or package resources in such a way that would give rise to higher values, how can we be sure that the items would be, instantaneously or eventually, in the hands of the highest-value user to realize their higher values? To sell a product or a property, one needs to locate another party who has a higher valuation than his or her own and can afford to pay for the acquisition. Similarly, to acquire an item, one needs to have the financing capability and find an owner who is attaching a valuation lower than him or her on the item.[39] If a property is transferred to a user who attaches to or could derive from the property a higher value, a gain could be made. On the incentive, and also the limit, of possible gains, an individual would search for parties who assign valuations higher than his or hers on his or her own property, or locate properties or rights of use selling at prices lower than the values he or she could derive from them.[40] When the property is in the hands of the highest-value user, no more gain from exchange is possible and the level of collective gain is also maximized. A community where such searches are unhindered but rewarded is thereby best positioned to move to its best possible state.[41]

USE VALUE AND OWNERSHIP VALUE

A property needs not be owned by the highest-value user to generate the highest value, as the highest-value user may simply rent or buy the rights of use from the owner. However, in contemplating whether to sell a property, an owner compares the current ownership value (which is taken to be the value he or she as an owner can derive from a property without putting it into use himself or herself, or the value that he or she could obtain from the users as the owner of the property) and the buying price being offered

---

39 The difference in value between a good that entails only personal affection to one party and one that has a strong commercial appeal worldwide lies not only in the size of the pool of persons who see it as valuable, but also how well-endowed they are. Obviously, the larger the pool is and the richer those in the pool are, the greater the chance that the exchange value is higher.

40 The same incentives drive searches for differences in valuation on properties by deal makers who do not own the properties before and perhaps not even during the search process.

41 Whether by reselling or for one's own use, exchange is a matching exercise of individuals' valuations and affordability. Not only is making a valuation an individual-based matter and contingent on one's perception, the attainments of a better state of well-being or realizations of higher levels of value via exchanges are also contingent on the valuations and capabilities of other parties, which determine how much extra benefit or value can be derived for the community (with the exchange value determining the distribution of the gain).

by an interested party, who forms his or her offer price based on owner-ship value projected on the usage charge he or she expects to receive from the users of the property as the owner. Therefore, use value and ownership value are essentially a distributional matter, as is further illustrated by the example below of cows grazing on privately owned land.

To keep it simple, we assume that the only use value that could be de-rived from the piece of land is the appreciation in the value of the cows be-ing reared on it. If the cows belong to the landowner, the ownership value of the property equals the sum of the use value generated, which equals, as assumed, the appreciated value of the cows.

Now suppose the landowner rents his property to some cow raisers to collect rental income instead. The ownership value as such becomes the sum of the rental income, appropriately discounted and aggregated. Assuming further that what is needed to rear the cows wholly comes from the land and is included in the rental, what the tenant would get is the ap-preciated value of the cows net of the total rental paid.

If the tenant cow raisers pay a rental that is the total appreciated value of their cows, then they would make no net gain. The resulted ownership value to the landowner would be the same as that in the case where he is the cow raiser as well, assuming the tenant and the landowner achieve the same productivity in cow rearing. In other words, the lower the rental the tenants manage to bargain from the landowner, the larger the portion of use value they can retain and the larger their net gains would be. That evidently implies that the ownership value would be lower accordingly, which in turn suggests that the rental and ownership value is primarily a distributional issue.

Would transferability affect the value of the land? More specifically, would a property become worthless if the ownership right is nontransfer-able? If an owner does not raise cows, a nontransferable ownership right does not prevent the property from being deployed to its highest-value use. As spelled out above, the owner could simply rent the land to the high-est-value user. As long as the net benefit from renting the land (i.e., the appreciation in value netted against rental payable) is still the best among the available options, the prospective tenant cow raiser will be willing to rent the right of use from the landlord, giving the land a positive owner- ship value.

In fact, the contract could be packaged as a perpetual lease in return for a lump-sum payment, making it materially similar to the sale of the own- ership rights. Alternatively, the owner could simply employ the one who knows how to deliver the highest value to manage or work on his property (i.e., to rear cows as in the current example), just like in the earlier example where the Subordinate pays rentals or receives wages. In short, nontrans- ferability does not necessarily consign a zero ownership value to the land.

THE DIFFERENCE COST CAN MAKE

Whether a property carries a positive ownership value therefore depends on neither the owner being a user nor the ownership right being transfer- able. Only when no one, not even the owner, can find any way to generate value from a property (such that the property has no use value at all) would the property have a zero ownership value. But does this suggest that a property with a positive use value always commands a positive ownership value? Could it be the case that the ownership of a property yielding a positive use value is worthless or, worse, a liability?

For that to be the case, the owner must not be able or willing to col- lect any rent from the cow raisers. Suppose the use of the property is free of charge or that the amount of the charge is fixed regardless of the usage, meaning that there is no additional charge for a cow to eat more grass. In this case, a cow raiser would let the cow graze until further intake makes the cow sick (i.e., the return on that extra unit of intake is negative). In contrast, if the charge is calculated on the basis of the amount of grass consumed, one would stop letting the cow graze when the expected rise in value of the cow for taking in one more unit of grass is less than the corresponding unit charge. As such, consumption of grass on a commonly owned prop- erty without charge or with a lump-sum charge is typically higher than that where a consumption-based charge is levied. Nevertheless, as long as the consumption-based charge is not at such a high level that no one could feed the cows profitably, the cow raisers would still be willing to pay the landowner in order to have the cows fed at a profit.

However, how is the charge collected? First of all, those who have paid and those who have not need to be differentiable. Secondly, those caught trespassing must be made to pay a penalty that exceeds the prescribed consumption charge in order to make the charging scheme credible. Thirdly, the total of the collected charges netted against the cost of the whole charge-collection scheme (e.g., for identifying and differentiating users, expelling trespassers, measuring usage, and collecting fees accordingly) cannot be worse than the expected loss if entry is unrestricted or trespasses are left unchecked. Otherwise, opening the property to all is a better option than implementing the charging scheme, or tolerating trespasses is the preferred option.

In other words, even if positive use values could be derived from a property, when the rent or charge collectible from users is inadequate to cover the cost of running the charging regime, it may not be worthwhile to charge the users. With no income that can be collected, this will result in a zero ownership value for the property. Worse, if the users can potentially inflict damages as a result of their activities on the owner's property and it is also too costly for the owner to reclaim the damages from the users or to expel them, owning the property may become a liability. That is to say, even if some party is able to generate a positive use value from a property, it does not necessarily follow that the property commands a positive ownership value. Having a positive use value only meets the necessary condition but not the sufficient condition for a property to have a positive ownership value.

By the same token, a property does not have to be individually owned to have a positive ownership value. A commonly owned property or a property that belongs to everyone or a group of designated persons among whom no one is given the right to exclude others[42] (often associated with

---

42 Although no exclusive ownership right is granted to any individual, the right to the gain that an individual could derive from the use of the property remains vested with him or her. For instance, the consequential rise in value of a cow of yours that grazes on a commonly owned land remains yours. The question is whether you have to pay for the usage.

unrestricted usage) does not have to end up in a zero or negative ownership value. The owners of a commonly owned property may render it worthwhile to act collectively to appoint a steward to enact a consumption-based fee-collection scheme that limits the consumption or usage among themselves and share the net proceeds collected, as long as the cost of administering and enforcing the scheme is not prohibitively high. As a variant, if the cost to measure consumption or usage is prohibitively high but the cost of entry control is not, the owners may then choose to charge an entry fee or lump-sum payment for unrestricted consumption (similar to the charging scheme for buffets). The owners could still capture a portion of the use value from the users, entailing the property a positive ownership value.

In short, for a property to have a positive ownership value, we need to have all of the following:

1. The property has a positive use value.
2. The owner is able to pocket a portion of the use value from the users.
3. The proceeds exacted from the users are sufficient to cover the cost of doing so.
4. The users after paying the charge are still sufficiently incentivized to make use of the property.

The above outlines how the value derived from making use of a property may be distributed between the user and the owner, and illustrates the difference that the cost of collecting the usage fee from the users could make to the ownership value of a property. No matter what role, if any, the owner plays in bringing forth or altering the size of the use value, a property with a positive use value does not necessarily carry a positive ownership value when cost considerations set in.

10

Competition Intensity as a Strategic Variable

As the preceding discussion shows, for analyses on competition intensity as a strategic variable in decision making (as exemplified by the maneuvers to fence or to foster competition), the asymmetric preference on competition intensity and the cost of putting the strategies into practice need to be put together to get a full picture. Applying this back to the medieval castle example, discussed in chapter 8, for instance, the Dominant may try to circumscribe the Subordinate to make it more costly for the latter to free ride on the use of the lands or to deal with the Outsider directly—which may require erecting castle walls, deploying patrols, and so forth. Yet those costs to fence off competition may become so high that it may be preferable for the Dominant to give the Subordinate a free hand in deciding to whom and at what price he sells his produce, similar to how the landowner found it not worthwhile to collect charges from the users. For simplicity, the different types of costs for defending one's property rights by curtailing competition will be hereafter referred to as "fencing cost."

As one would expect, different types of property give rise to different fencing cost attributes and schedules. Enforcing a fee-collection scheme on a vast and open grazing land in a sparsely inhabited area would be costly, for example. Preventing unauthorized lumbering on such a landscape is also likely to be costly. However, the cost of enforcing a fee-collection scheme is much lower for, say, a collectively owned investment scheme like a unit trust or mutual fund, where the ownership is typically "conditionally open," requiring the prospective investors or unitholders to make a certain amount of capital contribution and accept the applicable terms and conditions authorizing appointed managers to deploy the pooled capital for specified investment purposes, in return for financial gains (or losses) as a result of the managers' investment decisions.

Given that the unitholders do not have direct access to the funds, and that the pooled capital and the control on the use and distribution are in the hands of the appointed managers, the costs for collecting fees and for erecting effective fencing against unauthorized uses by the owners (i.e., the unitholders) are low. The consequential risk is more on the pooled capital being misappropriated by the managers than by the unitholders.[43] Generally, when the rights of use and of ownership are separated, the risk of misappropriation is more likely to originate from the party with the rights to deploy, apportion, or directly derive use value from the property.

With information on the applicable cost-and-benefit schedule, a self-interest individual could evaluate the effectiveness of the spending on fencing or fostering competition as a strategic option in securing the maximum benefit for oneself. As for fencing, for instance, when installing door locks, one may use some simple padlocks or install a state-of-the-art antitheft system. The higher level of security offered by the latter choice, which may not be able to block out all burglars anyway, calls for a higher resource outlay, and that higher cost may not be justifiable when weighed against the expected chance of professional burglars breaking in and the monetary value of the properties inside the premises.

The fencing tactics adopted by one spell different implications on the cost and benefit of the countertactics deployed by the other parties involved. A frontier general may defend his country by putting up heavy garrisons at commonly used gateways and less firepower along tougher routes, thereby raising the cost of attack via the common routes but in effect lowering the relative cost of the riskier ones. Adventurous commanders, when figuring counterfencing measures, may in turn take the rockier

---

43 This is customarily reduced by appointments of custodians and auditors.

route on that very rationale, like Hannibal and Napoleon, who crossed the Alps directly, when assessing the casualties of directly combating the opponents versus those of taking the ferocious route.

With each property having its own check-and-balance characteristics, and hence the corresponding benefits and costs of fencing and counterfencing, the objective is less, if at all, about enacting a perfect fencing or counterfencing but more on maximizing the net gain as a means of giving oneself a competitive advantage. One chooses the appropriate level or strategy of fencing or counterfencing to be enacted to wedge the expected extra cost burden on the counterparties, so as to give oneself the highest net benefit level.

PUTTING BENEFIT AND COST TOGETHER: THE POSSIBILITIES

Fencing Competition

Going back to the example, the Dominant in the medieval castle, after evaluating the benefits and costs of the different levels of fencing as a buyer, would enact what he thinks the most appropriate or beneficial level of fencing. The effects of the fencing on the Subordinate and the Outsider could be represented by the extra cost that either or both of them have to bear when transacting with the other. For the present purpose, the level of that higher transaction cost is hypothesized to depend on the level of fencing that the Dominant enacts and the effectiveness of the countermeasures that the Subordinate or the Outsider may deploy, singly or collectively. The more comprehensive the fencing is, the more costly it is for the Subordinate and the Outsider to transact with each other. On the contrary, the more effective the countermeasures are, the smaller the increase in the transaction cost or the lower the level of the transaction cost will be.

Since the consideration that the Subordinate is to receive is what is paid by the Outsider netted against the transaction costs borne by the Subordinate and the Outsider, and it is that net consideration that matters to the Subordinate's decisions, the Dominant may try to alter the decisions of the Subordinate by varying the intensity of fencing and hence the corresponding level of transaction costs.

As an illustration, suppose the Outsider is willing to pay $10 to buy a specified amount of produce from the Subordinate, and as an outsider, he has to pay $2 on his part to secure the transaction. The net offer to the Subordinate therefore is only $8. If the Subordinate himself has to spend another $4 to, say, establish trade links with the Outsider, he can only pocket a net amount of $4 in the end. That means the Dominant is paying a consideration that is slightly higher than $4 is sufficient to outbid the Outsider, giving him a near $6 advantage in bidding. Hence, the more costly it is to make the transaction, the smaller the net amount the Subordinate will receive and the smaller the amount the Dominant needs to pay to outbid the Outsider.

Unitary Effect

Suppose now that the Dominant decides to spend $20 on fencing, as shown in Scenario A in table 10.1. It is further supposed that fencing efficiency is unitary in the sense that the effect of that spending on others' transaction costs is the same amount as the fencing spending, implying that a $20 spending on fencing results in an extra transaction cost burden of $20 on the others. Also, assume that the effects fall evenly on the Outsider and the Subordinate, such that each pays $10 in transaction costs to trade with each other. After deducting the total transaction costs to be borne by himself and the Outsider (from the gross consideration that the latter is willing to pay for the produce), the net amount that the Subordinate pockets is $130.

To par with the Outsider, as mentioned, the Dominant needs to pay an amount that equals the net amount the Subordinate is to receive from the Outsider, which is $130. That brings the total cost for the Dominant—which is the sum of the fencing cost (i.e., $20) and the minimum bidding consideration (i.e., $130)—to $150 as well, the same as the gross amount the Outsider is willing to pay. We can see that in the case of unitary fencing effect and when fencing cost is included, the Dominant has no bidding advantage over the Outsider.

Table 10.1. The Dominant in Control?

	Scenarios				
	A Unitary Effect	B Multiplied Effect	C Different Allocation	D New Tech for Subordinate	E Free Competition
(1) Spending on fencing	($20)	($40)	($40)	($40)	$0
(2) Efficiency of fencing	1.0x	1.5x	3.0x	0.75x	-
(3) Resulted transaction cost (total)	($20)	($60)	($120)	($30)	-
(4) Extra cost to be borne by Outsider	($10)	($30)	$0	($30)	$0
(5) Max price the Outsider is willing to pay	$150	$150	$150	$150	$150
(6) Net price offered by Outsider (=(5)-(4))	$140	$120	$150	$150	$150
(7) Extra cost to be borne by Subordinate	($10)	($30)	($120)	($30)	$0
(8) Net price receivable by Subordinate (=(6)-(7))	$130	$90	$30	$120	$150
(9) Minimum purchase consideration to be paid by Dominant (=(8))	$130	$90	$30	$120	$150
(10) Gross cost advantage over Outsider (=(5)-(9))	$20	$60	$120	$30	$0
(11) Net benefit of fencing (=(10)-(1))	$0	$20	$80	($10)	$0
Decision: Enact fencing?	Indifferent	Yes	Yes	No	N/A

Varying Effects

Now suppose that perhaps due to economies of scale or some improvements in fencing technology, the Dominant achieves a multiplied effect when doubling the spending on fencing. Maintaining the assumption that each will bear half of the cost increase, the Outsider and the Subordinate now have to shoulder a transaction cost of $30 each, raising the total to $60, as spelled out in Scenario B. The net consideration receivable by the Subordinate, and hence the minimum price the Dominant has to pay, falls to $90. That reduces the minimum total outlays that the Dominant has to make (the sum of the fencing cost and the minimum bid) to $130, or $20 less than that by the Outsider, giving the Dominant an advantage of the same amount.

Fencing will be even more effective if the spending is more focused. By shifting his fencing spending to target on the Subordinate alone, as in Scenario C—such that the Outsider does not bear any transaction cost and the Subordinate, when trading with the Outsider, has to pay for the whole of the higher transaction cost that has now jumped to $120—the net consideration the Subordinate expects to receive from the Outsider drops to $30. A consideration from the Dominant slightly higher than $30 is therefore enough to induce the Subordinate to deal directly with him. After netting against the $40 spending on fencing, the Dominant is in command of a near $80 advantage over the Outsider.

The advantage, however, gets dissolved in Scenario D where, due to the availability of some leading-edge communications technology facilitating transactions between the Subordinate and the Outsider, the effect of the Dominant's fencing strategy is diluted. The Subordinate as a result only has to pay $30 in extra costs to trade with the Outsider, pocketing a net amount of $120 for the produce. The minimum total outlay for the Dominant, after spending $40 on fencing, rises to $160, relegating him to a disadvantaged position. It has become prohibitively costly for the Dominant to enact fencing to restrain competition.

If without the fencing factor such that competition is not restrained, as in Scenario E, neither the Dominant nor the Outsider would have a fencing-induced advantage over the other. Biddings between themselves would drive their bid prices to the valuations they have on the produce, which coincide at $150, or the assumed level of valuations that the Dominant and the Outsider place on the produce. As such, the Subordinate benefits from the higher price ($150) made possible by the more intense competition between the Dominant and the Outsider.

Therefore, the more effective fencing is (as represented by the higher ratio of total transaction cost wedged to the fencing cost incurred), the more beneficial it will be for the Dominant to enact fencing to circumscribe the Subordinate from other buyers. Equally, the less effective it is, the less worthwhile it is for him to fence.

Fostering Competition

As discussed in chapter 8, to protect himself against being trumped by the Subordinate, the Dominant may foster competition by enlarging his supply base such that he has more substitutes available and could preempt the threat that the Subordinate may put up against him. For illustrative purpose, it is assumed that the benefit the Dominant expects he can obtain from fostering competition among the suppliers will be captured by the savings in the purchase consideration for the produce.

To induce the formation of a larger supply base, the Dominant may need to incur extra costs, such as acquiring more lands to house the new subordinates or building warehouses for the additional produce. He may also link up with new supply sources in other places or subsidize, partially or wholly, the counterparties' transaction cost: for instance, by improving access to his castle for suppliers in the neighborhood so as to lower their cost to conduct business with him. Again, for simplicity, the resources deployed to foster competition are summarily labeled as "fostering cost."

Rows 1 to 5 of Scenario F and Scenario G in table 10.2 illustrate the basic benefit and cost of whether it is worthwhile to pursue propositions to foster competition. Scenario F, having assumed a unitary effect of the fostering spending, yields an indifferent result, while Scenario G shows a benefit of $25 if there is an initiative to foster competition.

Backfiring

Fostering competition, however, may also have ramifications on the level of fencing cost. For instance, with a larger mass of subordinates gathered on the Dominant's fostering strategy, it would be more costly to block them from dealing directly with the Outsider. Also, the larger mass of sellers may lure in more buyers, which would also raise the cost of fencing them from trading with one another. Reciprocally, the level of fencing spending is lifted in order to maintain the fencing effect at the previous level, the effectiveness of the fostering strategy may consequentially be compromised, as the sellers may find it more costly to trade with the Dominant.

Not surprisingly, the cost of possible backfires, when included in the calculations of the net benefit of the initiatives to foster or fence competition, may affect the decision on the strategy to be adopted, as further illustrated in row 6 through row 7 in table 10.2 below.

Table 10.2. Worthwhile to Foster?

	Scenarios	
	F Unitary Effect	G Multiplied Effect
(1) Cost of produce if only one Subordinate	$250	$250
(2) Spending on fostering competition	$50	$50
(3) Efficiency of fostering spending	1.0x	1.5x
(4) Resulted benefit (fall in cost of produce)	$50	$75
(5) Benefit from fostering (before extra fencing cost) (= (4) – (2))	$0	$25
(6) Extra fencing cost required due to backfiring	($20)	($40)
(7) Net benefit from fostering (= (5) + (6))	($20)	($15)
Decision: To foster competition?	No	No

With unitary efficiency, as represented in Scenario F, the $50 spending to foster competition could only bring forth a $50 fall in the cost of the produce acquired. However, to maintain the same fencing effect, the enlarged supply pool calls for extra spending on fencing of $20, yielding a net loss of $20 for the fostering initiatives.

The picture looks better for the Dominant in Scenario G, where his fostering initiatives yield multiplied effects. The $50 spending pulls down the cost of produce by $75 to $175, giving the Dominant a gain of $25 before counting the backfire effect on fencing cost—which, however, has to be topped up by $40 so as to maintain the same level of effectiveness. The net benefit on the fostering spending turns into a $15 loss. In other words, when the backfire fencing cost is taken into account as well, it may no longer be beneficial for the Dominant to foster competition among the sellers, even with multiplied efficiency.

Fencing and Fostering Together

The five scenarios in table 10.1 show that given a certain level of fencing efficiency, the Dominant can ascertain if it is worthwhile to fence off the Subordinate from the Outsider, while those in table 10.2 illustrate how worthwhile it is to foster competition on the counterparty markets given the various assumptions. Taking the decisions on fencing and fostering together, table 10.3 below shows the minimum levels of fencing and fostering outlays required of the Dominant, now as a seller, to engineer markets of a certain level of competition intensity, as represented by the maximum bidding consideration that the buyers need to pay to acquire his produce.

Table 10.3. How to Sell the Produce

	Scenarios			
	H	I	J	K
(1) Expected maximum bidding price	$250	$350	$150	$200
(2) Acquisition cost of the produce	($100)	($100)	($100)	($100)
(3) Required fostering cost	$0	($30)	$0	($30)
(4) Required fencing cost	($50)	($100)	$0	$0
(5) Net benefit/(loss)	$100	$120	$50	$70
Decision: Which one to choose?	-	√	-	-
	New Linkage Technology			
	L	M	N	O
(1) Expected maximum bidding price	$250	$350	$150	$200
(2) Acquisition cost of produce	($100)	($100)	($100)	($100)
(3) Required fostering cost	$0	($10)	$0	($10)
(4) Required fencing cost	($100)	($200)	$0	$0
(5) Net benefit/(loss)	$50	$40	$50	$90
Decision: Which one to choose?	-	-	-	√

Assume that, perhaps due to geographical complexities, only one buyer (i.e., the Outsider) will come to the Dominant's castle if there is no spending to foster competition. However, to prevent other sellers from coming to compete against him, the Dominant needs to spend $50 on fencing. The spending mix is represented by Scenario H in table 10.3. Under such a setting of no competition on the buyer's and seller's sides, the Dominant could sell his produce, assumed to have been acquired at $100, for $250, pocketing a gross gain of $150 and a net gain of $100.

Suppose the Dominant now conjectures that he may be able to earn more by making his castle accessible to all interested buyers. Assume that doing so requires a spending of $30 on fostering, as depicted in Scenario I. With more buyers around, however, it would be more costly to fence off other sellers. Suppose the fencing cost has to be increased to $100 to maintain its effectiveness. If the sales proceeds under such circumstances go up to $350, the Dominant could take in a net gain of $120 after netting off the $100 cost of produce, the $30 fostering cost, and the $100 fencing cost. However, if the Dominant does not spend any on fencing or fostering as in Scenario J, such that there is no competition on the buyer's side but intense competition among the sellers, the maximum sales proceeds that the Dominant could fetch drop to $150, giving him a net gain of $50 only.

How about if the Dominant engineers a market structure where both the buyer and the seller sides are competitive, giving him sales proceeds of $200? For that to be the case, the Dominant needs to spend nothing to fence off competition but $30 to foster it. After deducting the cost of the produce and the fostering cost, the Dominant obtains a net benefit of $70, as depicted in Scenario K.

Comparing the net benefit levels of the four top scenarios, the worst case is Scenario J where the Outsider faces no pressure from other buyers but the sellers are competing intensely with the Dominant and among themselves. The Dominant as a seller could earn $50 only. The best option is to fence off other sellers and engineer a pool of competing buyers by investing $100 and $30 on fencing and fostering competition, respectively. Sales proceeds jump to $350 under that setting, and despite the higher level of total expenditures, the Dominant could make a net gain of $120, which is the highest among the first four scenarios.

Effects of Improvements in Linkage Technology

Suppose some remarkable progress is made in communications and linkage technologies, bringing down the transaction cost. While it is likely that the fostering cost would fall, since establishing trade links has become cheaper, the improvements in communications technology could be a double-edged sword when the fencing cost is taken more into account. The Subordinate and the Outsider could link up more cost-effectively, such that fencing becomes more costly for the Dominant. Yet the Dominant's ability to fence may also improve by capitalizing on the technological progress. The net effect on fencing cost is therefore less clear-cut.

A summary of the possible effects of the technological progress on the various strategic options is given in the bottom section of table 10.3, where it is assumed that the Dominant has to spend more on fencing to cut off the links between the buyers and the sellers as a result of the improved communications technology. Here, fencing has become a more expensive tactic. Fencing off the sellers and luring in as many buyers as possible is no longer the most profitable option. Instead, it is more beneficial not to fence but rather to spend a certain amount on fostering competition, as represented in Scenario O, which yields the highest net gain of $90.

A MATTER OF DEGREE

The above illustrates the expected results from the various possible combinations of fencing and fostering competition. We have seen that to justify spending on fencing, it has to generate a multiplied effect so that the total extra transaction cost that is to be borne by others is greater than the spending on fencing (after taking into account the effects of backfiring, if any). This gives the Dominant an advantage over the competitors. Similarly, to foster competition, the expected fall in the cost of the produce for a buyer or the expected increase in sales consideration for a seller has to be more than enough to pay the fostering spending together with any increase in fencing cost due to backfiring. Evidently, given their interrelated nature, the two decisions should be a joint one.

The examples in the tables so far have been presented in discrete form. In practice, these decisions are more focused on magnitude or intensity. For instance, how much would one like to spend on protecting one's valuables? By installing a lock, a safe, or a central alarm system? Similarly, the security level of prisons is set with reference to the seriousness and violence level of the crimes committed by the criminals to be detained, which could be taken as a proxy measure of the perceived risk levels and the value of damage that could be avoided with the proper security measures. Corporations often also have their own budget allocations for the protection of their intellectual and physical property rights, as evaluated with reference to the value of the properties to be protected and the assessed risks and costs of protection. Makers of high-profit-margin luxurious products that may be readily counterfeited would be more willing to spend more on reclaiming the loss of revenue as a means of deterring competition from the counterfeits. Alternatively, shopping-mall owners or large-scale property developers might invest significantly to improve the access to their properties in order to raise the customer flow and the corresponding intensity of competition, thereby benefitting the shop tenants therein. In this case, the amount to be spent would be evaluated with reference to the expected increases in the selling price or the income yield of those properties.

In the next chapter, we will analyze, with the aid of diagrams, the decisions on fencing and fostering competition from a continuum perspective—or the choice over the *level* of spending put forth to fence and foster competition.

11

In an Integrated and
Continuum Context

THE DOMINANT AS A BUYER

Fencing Competition

In this chapter, we are going to use some basic supply-and-demand graphical analyses to illustrate, in an integrated and continuum context, the various possibilities of fencing and fostering strategies. Again, we will start with the Dominant's decision over fencing as a buyer, which is depicted below in figure 11.1.

Suppose there are two buyers, namely the Dominant and the Outsider. The "demand schedule" of each, or the maximum price one is willing to pay for each corresponding unit of the good, is represented by $D_D{}^0$ and $D_U{}^0$, respectively. The aggregate demand of the two is obtained by summing horizontally the two individual demand curves, denoted by the bolded line $D_A{}^0$. Since the quantity demanded by the Outsider becomes zero above the price level C, the Dominant becomes the sole buyer above that price level, and his demand curve in effect is the aggregate demand curve above that, giving rise to a kink at point B. Set against the supply curve of the Subordinate of $S_R{}^0$ (or the schedule of the minimum price at which he is willing to supply or sell the corresponding unit of good), the aggregate equilibrium is at $E_A{}^0$, where a total quantity of $Q_A{}^0$ units of the good is traded at price P^0. Appropriating back to the demand curves of the

Dominant and the Outsider at that price, the Dominant gets $Q_D{}^0$ units and the Outsider $Q_U{}^0$.

Figure 11.1.

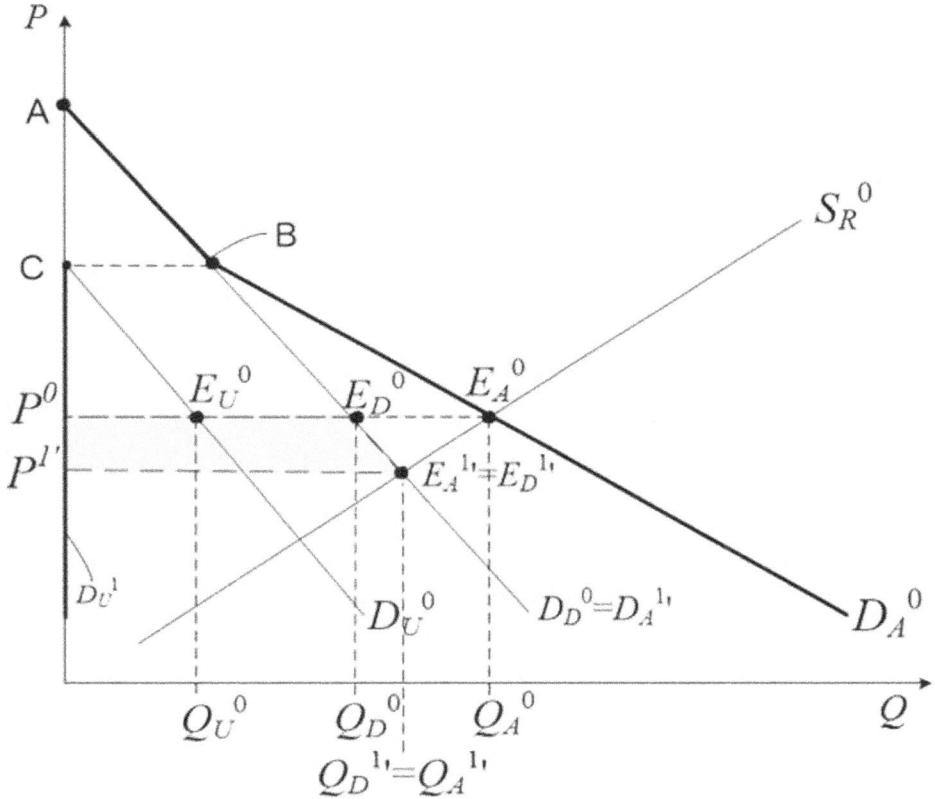

Suppose now the Dominant is to spend a certain amount on fencing (say, $F_D{}^1$), such that the extra cost wedged on the Outsider coincides exactly with his demand schedule. That means the net price that the Subordinate is to receive from the Outsider becomes zero for each and every unit of the good, which effectively prices the Outsider out of the market and nullifies his demand curve (i.e., $D_U{}^0$ shifted to the vertical line of $D_U{}^1$), making the demand curve of the Dominant the de facto aggregate demand curve, labeled as $D_A{}^{1}$'. The equilibrium shifts to $E_A{}^{1}$' correspondingly, where the price is brought down to P^{1}' and the quantity traded to $Q_A{}^{1}$', all of which going to the Dominant (i.e., $Q_A{}^{1}$' $= Q_D{}^{1}$').

How much does the Dominant gain? Without the fencing spending, the net gain the Dominant gets from the purchase or the excess of his valuation on the good netted against the price he pays (customarily called "consumer surplus" in economics) is represented by the area $AE_D{}^{0}P^0$. With the fencing spending, his consumer surplus increases to $AE_D{}^{1}$'P^{1}', which is larger than the initial size of consumer surplus by $P^0E_D{}^{0}E_D{}^{1}$'P^{1}'.

Allocation Effect

However, the above has not taken into account the effect of the fencing spending on the amount of resources available for purchases. Since the amount of resources at the disposal of the Dominant is fixed, allocating a portion of them to fencing reduces what is left for buying goods and hence the amount of the good that he can afford to buy from the Subordinate at every price level.

Graphically, that is represented by a leftward shift of the demand curve for the good, as shown in figure 11.2, by the shift of the Dominant's demand curve from $D_D{}^{0}$ to $D_D{}^{1}$. This is the "allocation-effect-augmented demand curve." Since the Outsider is priced out of the market, the final aggregate demand curve again coincides with that of the Dominant's, resulting in $D_A{}^{1}$ overlapping with $D_D{}^{1}$. The equilibrium as a result moves from $E_A{}^{0}$ to $E_A{}^{1}$, which is also where $E_D{}^{1}$ is.

We can see that the consumer surplus is smaller when the allocation effect is included ($CE_D{}^{1}P^1$ versus $AE_D{}^{1}$'P^{1}'). In fact, since the Dominant has a fewer amount of resources available for purchases after the fencing spending, the $E_A{}^{1}$' is hypothetical and for illustration only; in other words, it is not realizable in practice. The fall in the consumer surplus due to the allocation effect indeed could be taken as a representation of the value of loss or the cost of fencing to the Dominant.

Figure 11.2.

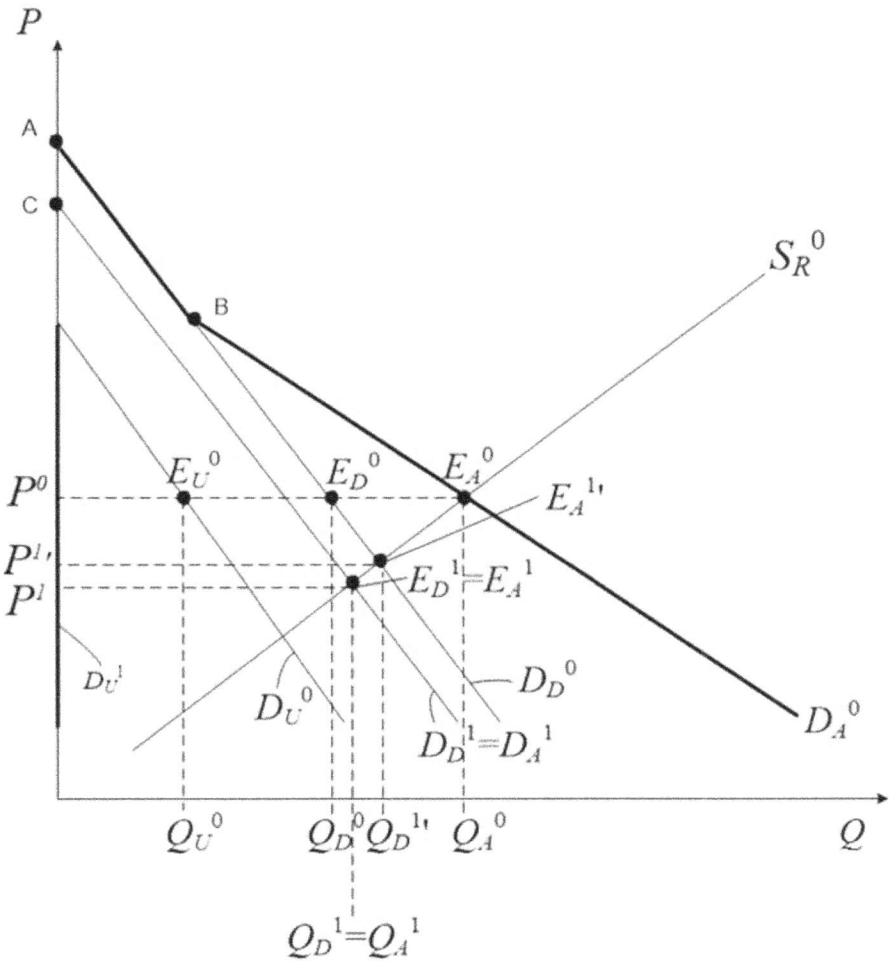

While the gain to the Dominant when the allocation effect is included will be smaller, does that render fencing no longer a beneficial choice to the Dominant? If the shifted demand curve is parallel to the initial one, as assumed in the current case, then the two consumer surplus areas are similar triangles. Their relative sizes can therefore be ascertained simply by comparing any one corresponding pair of their lengths. Whether fencing could bring in a larger gain can thus be determined by whether the Dominant could acquire more of the good after incurring the fencing spending, or whether $Q_D{}^1$ is longer than $Q_D{}^0$, which happens to be the case in the current illustration.

To Fence Less

What if the Dominant reduces his fencing spending? For the Dominant, with a smaller spending on fencing the allocation effect will be smaller, and thus his demand curve will shift less to the left accordingly. However, on a smaller fencing spending, the Outsider will have his bidding power only partially blocked and will not be priced out completely. That is, the Subordinate is to receive, in net terms, a positive price from the Outsider. The resulting Outsider's demand curve would hence be somewhere in between the completely blocked-out demand curve of $D_U{}^1$ on the vertical axis and his unblocked demand curve of $D_U{}^0$.

The last two scenarios have been graphed in figure 11.3, where $D_D{}^1$ remains the representation of the complete priced-out case, while $D_D{}^2$ shows the partial case, both for the Dominant. The partially blocked demand curve of the Outsider is represented by $D_U{}^2$. The aggregate demand curve shifts to $D_A{}^2$ correspondingly, bringing the equilibrium quantity and price level to $Q_A{}^2$ and P^2, respectively.

Figure 11.3.

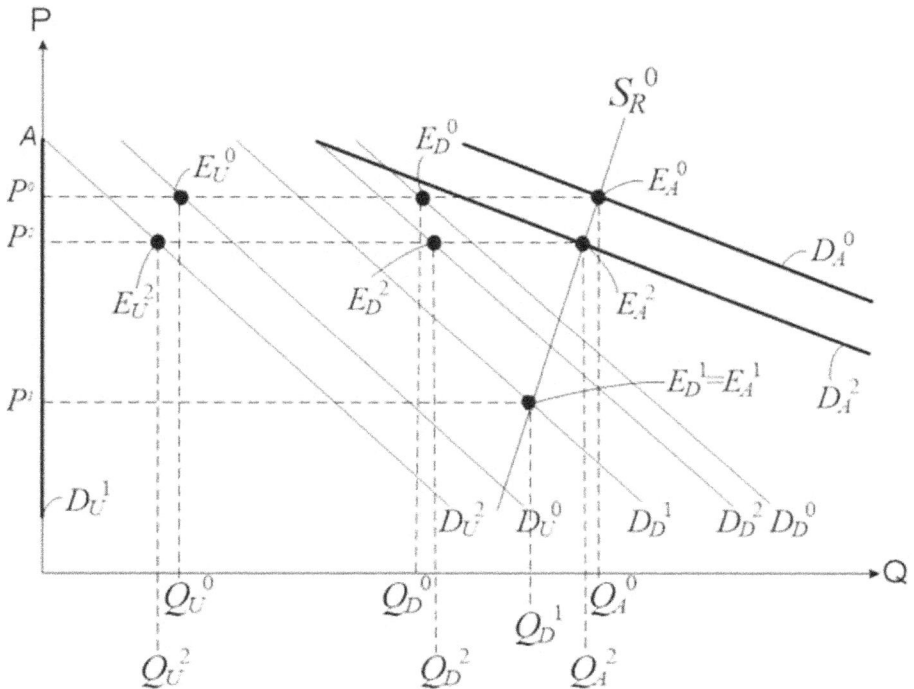

In terms of distribution, by comparing the various quantities of the good acquired (i.e., Q_D^0, Q_D^1, and Q_D^2), we can deduce that the consumer surplus attributable to the Dominant in the partially blocked case is greater than that in the unblocked case, but less than that in the complete priced-out case. The gain to the Outsider, in contrast, improves from nothing to a size represented by the area of $AE_U^2P^2$.

The Optimal Level

We can therefore see that each level of fencing spending has its corresponding level of consumer surplus. The $FEff_D^1$ curve in figure 11.4 plots out an example of the relationship of the two, which basically involves the efficiency of fencing in bringing forth gain attributable to the Dominant as represented by the level of his consumer surplus.

Figure 11.4.

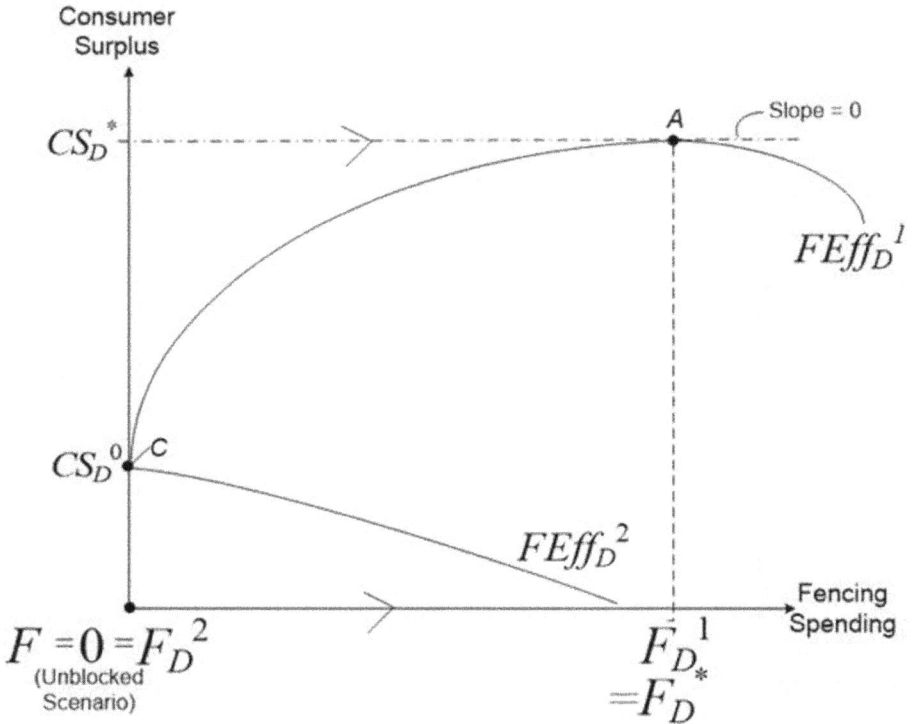

In the example above, F_D^1 is the level of fencing spending that completely blocks out the Outsider. For fencing spending beyond that level, the size of consumer surplus to the Dominant shrinks. This means the level of fencing spending F_D^1 represents the level that gives the maximum level of consumer surplus that the Dominant can get from his fencing initiatives, unless the Dominant is able to squeeze out more from the Outsider or the Subordinate or both for a fencing spending beyond F_D^1—such that the Dominant is in effect subsidized by the other two. In other words, it is the optimal level of fencing spending to him, denoted as F_D^*.

In terms of cost-and-benefit analysis, by spending more than F_D^* to fence competition, the size of the gain decreases, suggesting that the additional or the marginal unit of fencing spending reduces the gain. This means that the corresponding change in consumer surplus or the marginal consumer surplus of that unit is negative. Similarly, if the Dominant reduces his fencing spending when total spending is below F_D^*, his total net consumer surplus will also fall, implying that the marginal unit of fencing spending being chopped off is indeed a net contribution to the total, or that the marginal consumer surplus is positive.

Putting the two strands together, the Dominant (or any individual) will continue to increase fencing spending as long as the marginal benefit of fencing, after the allocation effect is included, is positive and will stop short of the level where the marginal benefit becomes negative. For the reverse, an individual will keep reducing the fencing spending if the marginal benefit of fencing is negative until reaching the unit of fencing that brings a positive contribution to the total size of gain. It suggests that the Dominant will attain the maximum level of gain when the marginal benefit of fencing equals zero, constituting the optimal level of fencing spending by the Dominant.

Since the marginal benefit at each level of fencing is the change in the total consumer surplus relative to the change in total fencing spending, graphically this is represented by the corresponding slope of the *FEff* curve at that level of fencing spending, or the slope of the tangent line drawn on the *FEff* curve at that level of fencing spending. The optimal level of fencing spending is therefore represented by where the slope of the tangent line equals zero, or that of a horizontal line. In figure 11.4, that occurs at point A, where the slope of the tangent line drawn on $FEff_D^1$ at that level of fencing spending equals zero. Expectedly, point A coincides with the optimal level of fencing spending of F_D^*.

However, fencing may not always be effective. If the Dominant is unable to attain a higher level of consumer surplus at any level of fencing spending, the $FEff$ curve will be everywhere below the initial level of consumer surplus where no fencing spending is made, as denoted by CS_D^0 in the figure. Since any positive level of fencing spending puts the Dominant in a position worse than where no fencing is made, he is not incentivized to make any.

An example of that is given by $FEff_D^2$. As it is everywhere below the initial level of CS_D^0, a corner solution will be resulted at point C where no fencing spending will be made (i.e., $F_D^2 = 0$), with the consumer surplus remaining at CS_D^0.

We can see that whether the Dominant will make any fencing spending at all as well as what level of spending he will pursue depends on how much net gain he expects he will obtain from the spending. Here, he will take into account the allocation effect of the fencing spending on his own purchasing power as well. In other words, it is the expected return or productivity of the fencing spending that matters to the Dominant.

A Pareto Change?

A collective or a society is said to be at a "Pareto optimum" when there can be no more change conceivable that makes a party better off without making some other party worse off. Reciprocally, when such a change is possible, it means there could be a Pareto improvement. In that context, is fencing a Pareto improvement for the society?

The society, as assumed in the current case, encompasses only three parties: the Dominant, the Outsider, and the Subordinate.

Figure 11.5.

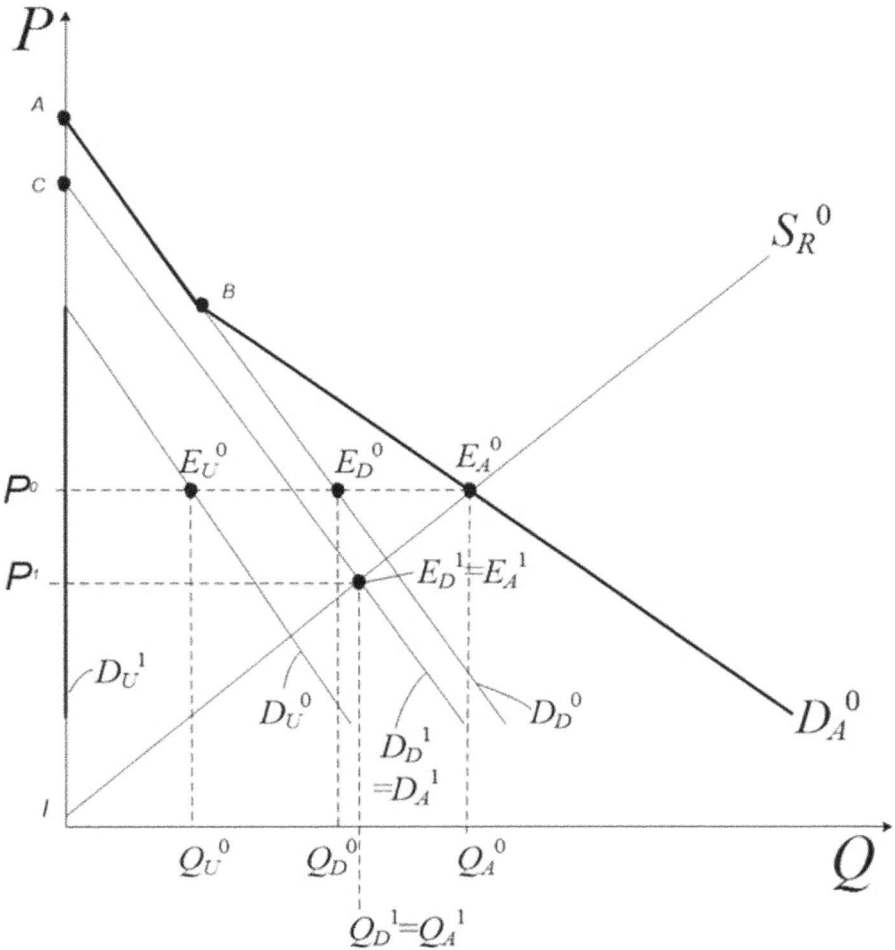

Aggregately speaking, the social gain without fencing amounts to the area $ABE_A{}^0I$ in figure 11.5, with the area below $P^0E_A{}^0$ attributable to the Subordinate (customarily known as the "producer surplus") and that above to the Dominant and the Outsider (the former getting the area $AE_D{}^0P^0$ and the latter $BE_A{}^0E_D{}^0$).

As mentioned, as the fencing spending cuts the size of resources available for purchases, the Dominant's demand curve is shifted from D_D^0 to D_D^1. The fencing spending reduces the quantity exchanged to Q_A^1 and hence the size of social gain to CE_A^1I, which is smaller than the initial size of the social gain. However, that fencing spending brings the Dominant a larger size of consumer surplus (area $CE_D^1P^1$ versus area $AE_D^0P^0$, or as can be ascertained by comparing the lengths of Q_D^1 and Q_D^0). The Outsider, on the contrary, loses all his share of the consumer surplus as a result of the fencing. The Subordinate's producer surplus shrinks from $P^0E_A^0I$ to $P^1E_A^1I$. Part of these losses finances the fencing spending and the net increase in consumer surplus for the Dominant, with the rest benefiting no one else. In aggregate, the society suffers from a social gain that is smaller by the area of $ABE_A^0E_D^1C$.

The Dominant is a beneficiary from his fencing spending. The Outsider, however, is priced out and gets nothing, and the Subordinate suffers as his size of producer surplus shrinks, rendering them both losers as a result of the Dominant's fencing spending. The fencing maneuver therefore violates the Pareto-optimum condition, as the gain to the Dominant is premised on the losses of the Outsider and the Subordinate. Even if compensation is viable and enforced, the move remains a deviation from the Pareto improvement since the society suffers a net loss, implying that the gain to the Dominant is insufficient to compensate for the losses suffered by the Outsider and Subordinate. Yet, since the Dominant pockets more, he is incentivized to go forward with the fencing, despite the losses for others.[44]

Fostering Competition

Figure 11.6 illustrates the other tactical strand that could be deployed by the Dominant as a buyer: to induce competition on the supply side.

---

44 The Outsider and the Subordinate can prevent that from happening by enacting countermeasures or by buying out the Dominant by offering him an amount greater than his net gain from fencing. Graphically, that could be represented by the ability of the Dominant to chip into the consumer surplus and the producer surplus of the Outsider and the Subordinate (which each could respectively pocket in the unblocked case). That may be achieved by means of multitier pricing levied by the Dominant on the other two parties. Whatever the tactics deployed by the Dominant, the rationale stays the same: to put up a level of actual or threatened fencing that maximizes his net gain.

Figure 11.6.

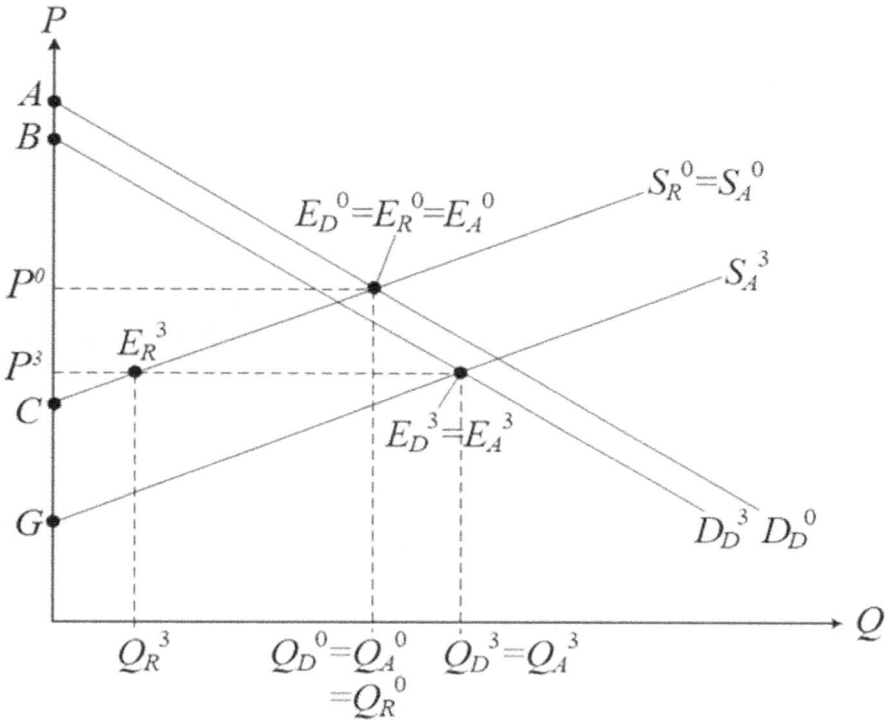

Now assume that the fostering spending could lure in more suppliers. With more suppliers bidding for the Dominant's business, the resulted price for each level of good is likely to fall. Put differently, the quantity of the good supplied at each price is likely to be larger. That is represented graphically by a rightward shift in the supply curve from S_A^0 (which coincides with that of the Subordinate as represented by S_R^0) to S_A^3, which is the aggregate of the supply curves of the Subordinate as well as other suppliers coming to the local market as a result of the Dominant's fostering spending. Demand curve of the Dominant shifts leftward as the fostering spending chops off a certain amount of resources available for purchases.

Assuming there is no outside buyer, the equilibrium as a result moves from E_A^0 to E_A^3, where the Dominant can buy more of the good ($Q_D^3 = Q_A^3 > Q_D^0 = Q_A^0$) and at a lower price ($P^3 < P^0$). The Subordinate, in contrast, produces less (Q_R^0 down to Q_R^3) and gains less (a producer surplus of the area $P^0E_R^0C$ versus area $P^3E_R^3C$, with the difference being represented by the shaded area). However, we have some new beneficiaries—the new entrants—who collectively pocket a gain of the area of $CE_R^3E_A^3G$. Society as a whole moves to a better position, as shown by the larger triangle of BE_A^3G against that of AE_A^0C.

Countermeasures (Outsider and Subordinate)

Would the Outsider or the Subordinate stand passive to the maneuvers of the Dominant? On the same decision-making model, each will adopt measures that deliver themselves the best levels of net benefit, given the knowledge that the other will act in the same manner.

Take the Outsider as an example. He is aware that the Dominant will enact fencing measures to prevent him from bidding for the good if it is beneficial to do so. The Outsider will evaluate the benefit that he may get from pursuing any countermeasures that would resist or dampen the effectiveness of the Dominant's fencing against the cost of putting up those countermeasures in order to decide on the best strategy for himself.

Suppose the Outsider's countermeasures are in the form of counter-fencing, which could dilute the effect of the Dominant's fencing spending. Graphically, that could be translated into a smaller leftward shift of his demand, as shown in figure 11.7 below.

Figure 11.7.

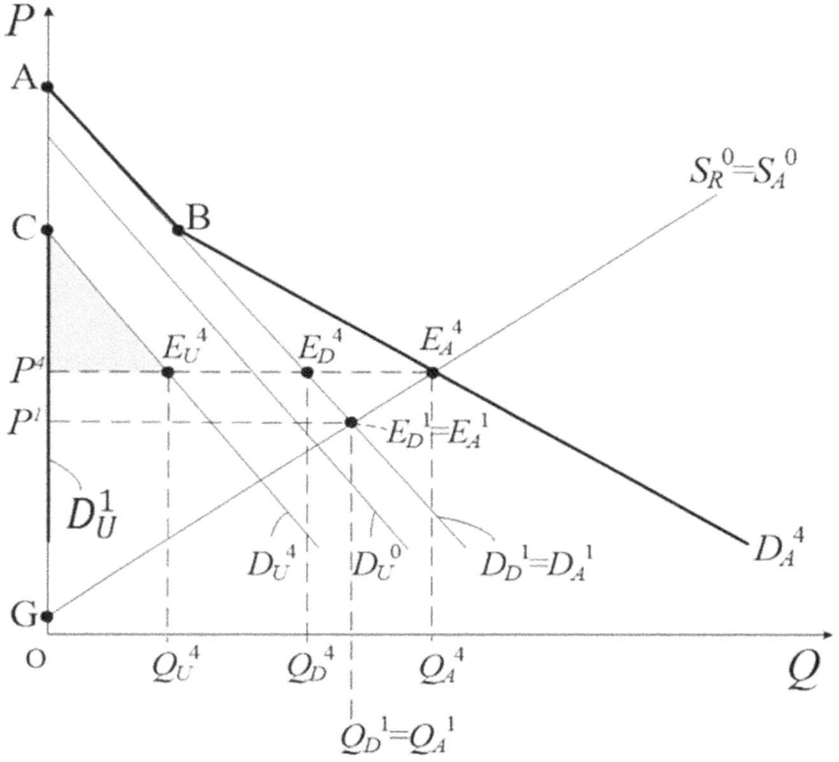

Instead of being completely forced out of play (D_U^1), the Outsider's counterfencing keeps him in the market, even though the leverage he has is still smaller than that in the unblocked case (D_U^0). D_U^4 represents his postcountermeasures demand schedule with the allocation effect included, whereas D_D^1 is the demand curve of the Dominant given his level of fencing spending. The new aggregate demand curve—which is the horizontal summation of the postcounterfencing demand curve of the Outsider (D_U^4) and postfencing demand curve of the Dominant (D_D^1)—is captured by D_A^4.

Market equilibrium moves from E_A^1 (where no counterfencing is implemented against the complete blocked-out fencing created by the

Dominant) to E_A^4, resulting in higher quantity exchanged and price. Saved from being wiped out and getting nothing, the Outsider acquires Q_U^4 units of the goods at price P^4 and pockets a consumer surplus of the shaded area of $CE_U^4P^4$. As for the Dominant, his equilibrium moves from E_D^1, where the Outsider pursues no counterfencing, to E_D^4, where the Outsider does counteract. He will get a smaller size of consumer surplus in view of the amount of goods he gets being down from Q_D^1 to Q_D^4. The loss is represented by the area of $P^4E_D^4E_D^1P^1$. The collective moves to a better position on the counterfencing (area ABE_A^4G versus area AE_A^1G).

The Outsider will compare the various levels of consumer surplus expected against the corresponding costs of the countermeasures so as to deduce the best strategy. An example of the relationship between the two has been plotted in figure 11.8, again in the form of a fencing efficiency curve that has been labeled as $FEff_U^4$.

Figure 11.8.

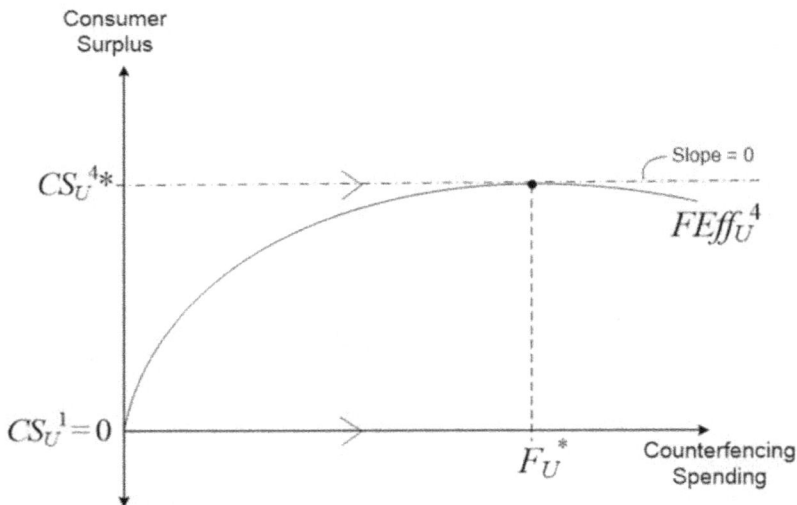

The level of consumer surplus of CS_U^1 represents the situation where the Outsider spends nothing on counterfencing and is completely blocked out. F_U^* is the optimal choice of counterfencing for the Outsider, as his consumer surplus is at the maximum at that level of counterfencing, as suggested by the longest vertical distance between the $FEff_U^4$ curve and the horizontal axis or the fact that the slope of the tangent line on the $FEff_U^4$ curve equals zero there.

Would countermeasures by the Subordinate also bring in beneficial results for himself and the collective? Suppose the Subordinate pursues countermeasures that dilute the dampening effect of the Dominant's fencing spending on the demand of the Outsider. That is, the Outsider's demand will be partially unblocked to the benefit of the Subordinate, as exemplified in figure 11.9, by the shift of the Outsider's demand curve from being completely blocked out (D_U^1) to partially so (D_U^5), and the corresponding shift of the aggregate demand curve from D_A^1 to D_A^5.

Figure 11.9.

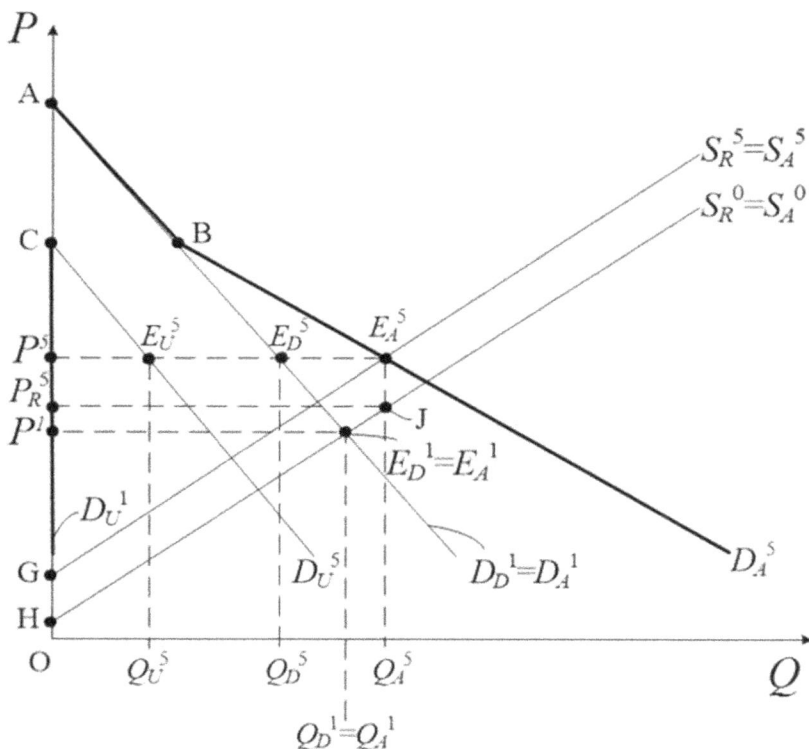

The allocation effect of the countermeasures by the Subordinate is represented by a parallel upward shift of his supply curve from S_R^0 to S_R^5, equivalent to a higher cost for every quantity level of the good supplied. The aggregate equilibrium accordingly moves from E_A^1 to E_A^5, with the quantity exchanged being increased from Q_A^1 to Q_A^5. The Dominant, however, suffers, as he can only acquire a smaller amount of the good (Q_D^5 versus Q_D^1) and pockets a smaller size of consumer surplus (area $AE_D^5P^5$ versus area $AE_D^1P^1$). The Outsider, as his demand resurfaces, gets Q_U^5 units of the good and obtains a consumer surplus of the size of $CE_U^5P^5$, rather than nothing.

The Subordinate sells Q_A^5 units of the good at a unit price of P^5. However, for each unit of the good, a certain amount of it is used to finance the countermeasure spending, which is represented by the vertical distance between S_R^5 and S_R^0, such that the net unit price he receives for selling the Q_A^5 units of the good is only P_R^5. Nevertheless, he still obtains a producer surplus that is larger by the area of $P_R^5 J E_A^1 P^1$.

Alternatively, apart from working on the buyer's side, the Subordinate may counteract by resisting the Dominant's fostering initiatives to expand the supply base. Recall the fostering campaign conducted by the Dominant as depicted in figure 11.6, where the aggregate supply curve moves from S_R^0 (when the Subordinate is the only supplier in the market) to S_A^3 (when additional suppliers are brought in), and the Dominant's demand curve shifts to D_D^3 due to the allocation effect of the fostering spending. The social equilibrium moves to E_A^3, with the price down to P^3 and quantity of the goods exchanged up to Q_A^3. The equilibrium of the Subordinate shifts to E_R^3.

Now suppose that to mitigate the effect of the Dominant's fostering campaign, the Subordinate contemplates engaging in a countercampaign to raise the cost level of the outside suppliers. As in figure 11.10, the aggregate supply curve shifts to S_A^6 instead of S_A^3, resulting in an equilibrium of E_A^6 but not E_A^3, which corresponds to a higher price of P^6 and a lower quantity of exchange of Q_A^6.

Figure 11.10.

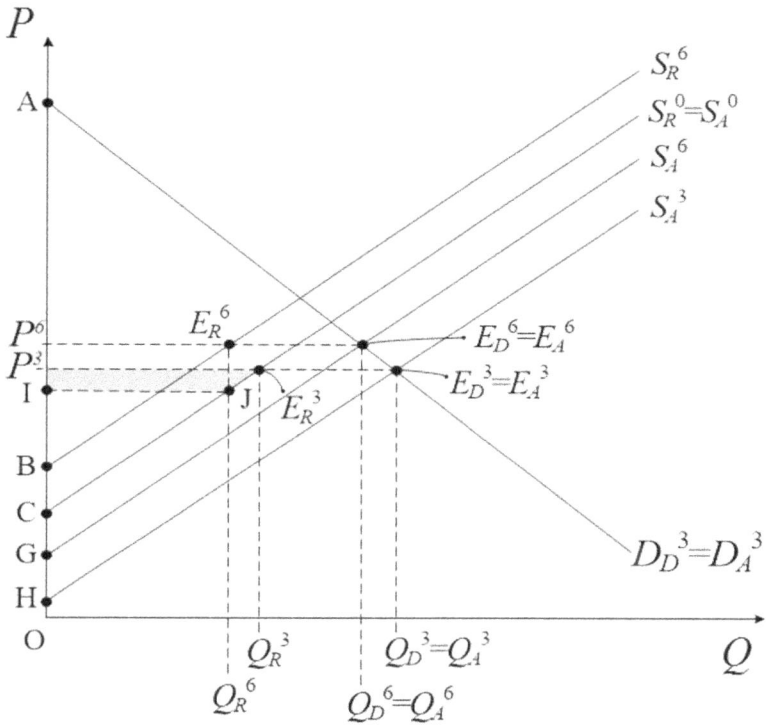

As the Subordinate's cost structure would become less competitive after making the countermeasures against the Dominant's fostering initiatives (as represented by his supply curve moving from S_R^0 to S_R^6) his take of the quantity exchanged would fall from Q_R^3, where no countermeasures are undertaken, to Q_R^6. The size of his producer surplus would also shrink after accounting for the allocation effect of the countermeasure spending (area $P^3E_R^3C$ versus area $P^6E_R^6B$, which is the same size as IJC). That suggests that the Subordinate, given the expected payoffs above, will refrain from pursuing the countermeasures.

The collective would also suffer as the aggregate gain would be smaller (area AE_A^6G versus AE_A^3H) should the Subordinate pursue the blocking countermeasure. The consumer surplus attributed to the Dominant would also fall by the area of $P^6E_D{}^6E_D{}^3P^3$. The net effect on the other suppliers is less certain, however, and depends on whether the negative effect of the reduction in the quantity of the good sold by them is more than netted off by the positive contribution of the price increase.

THE DOMINANT AS A SELLER

To Block Other Sellers

The role as a seller for the Dominant is more or less the reciprocal of him as a buyer as discussed earlier. The corresponding strategic options include fencing competition on the supply side and fostering competition on the demand side, with the same objective: to maximize his net benefit. Two graphical illustrations are presented below.

Figure 11.11.

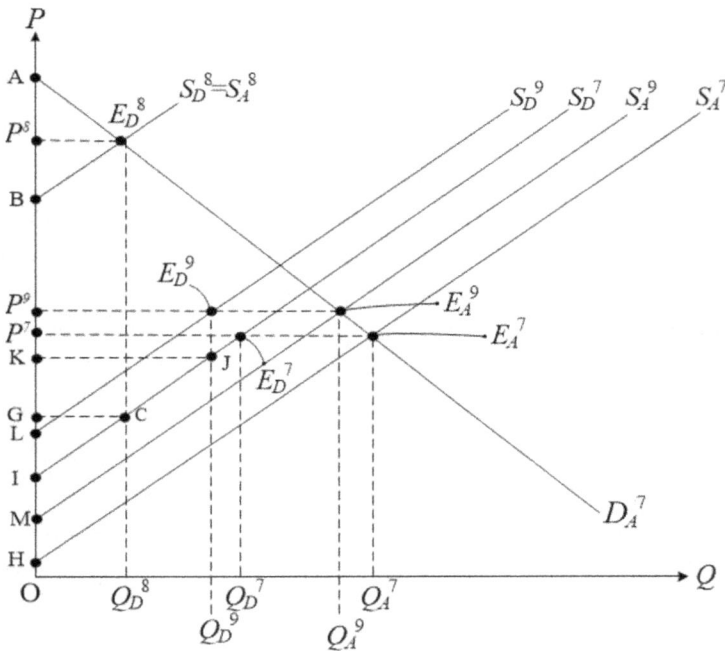

The example, as exemplified in figure 11.11, captures the basic decision setting for the Dominant as to how much he will fence competition on the supply side. Given his initial supply curve of S_D^7 and the market supply of S_A^7, set against the market demand of D_A^7, his initial position is at E_D^7 where he supplies Q_D^7 units of the total traded quantity of Q_A^7 units, all at the price of P^7.

Suppose by expending an amount of F_D^8 on fencing, other suppliers are completely blocked out, making his supply curve that of the whole market. That is represented by the shift from S_D^7 to S_D^8, which is his allocation-effect augmented curve and also the market supply curve of S_A^8. Market equilibrium moves to E_D^8, corresponding to a quantity exchanged of Q_D^8 and a price of P^8. Although the Dominant gets the whole market and the price has gone up, his size of the producer surplus has indeed become smaller (area $P^8E_D^8B$, which is the same size of GCI versus $P^7E_D^7I$), as the effective net price he receives drops to G due to the fencing spending. That is, complete fencing makes the Dominant worse off.

Given the results, suppose the Dominant considers retracting his fencing intensity to F_D^9, which exacts a smaller size of allocation effect on his cost base, bringing his supply curve to a less leftward position of S_D^9. The other suppliers are also not completely blocked out as a result, creating a market supply curve of S_A^9. Together, they yield a market equilibrium of E_A^9, which maps to a market price of P^9 and a total quantity traded of Q_A^9. That entails Q_D^9 units and a larger producer surplus to the Dominant (area $P^9E_D^9L$ or KJI versus area $P^8E_D^8B$ or GCI).

Whatever the level of fencing chosen by the Dominant, as long as it is effective in restraining the total supply, the collective moves to a worse-off position (area AE_A^7H versus area AE_D^8B versus area AE_A^9M). However, as in the case where the Dominant is a buyer, the consequence of bringing the collective to a worse-off scenario may be insufficient to dissuade the Dominant from enacting fencing as long as he expects that doing so will give him the best level of individual benefit in net terms.

Fostering Demand-Side Competition

The Dominant may also foster competition on the demand side such that the engineered increase in demand could become a net gain for himself. Assume, for simplicity, there is no other supplier in the market and that a fostering campaign of the cost of F_D^{10} will result in an expansion in demand from D_A^7 to D_A^{10} as graphed out in figure 11.12.

Figure 11.12.

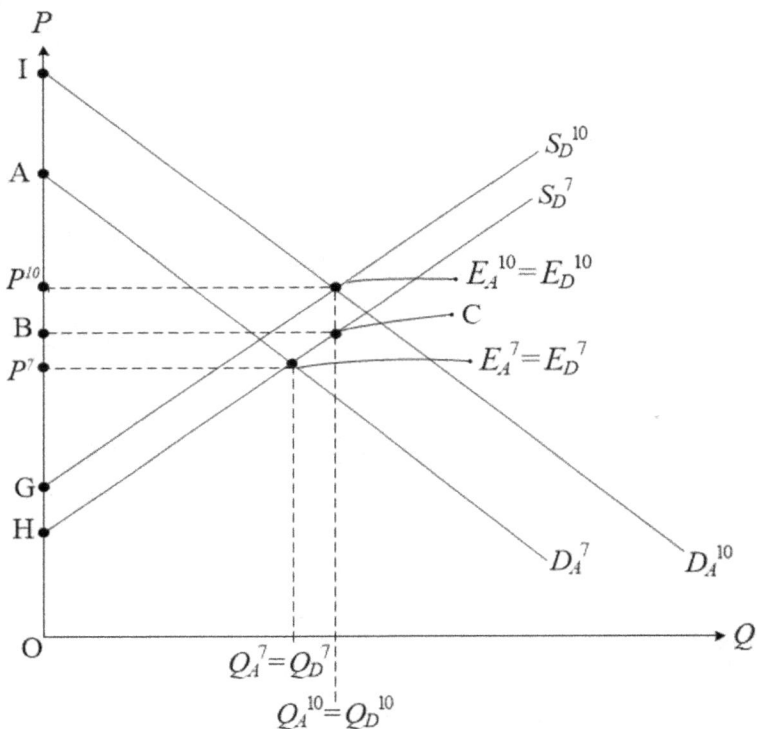

After accounting for the allocation effect of the fostering spending, we can see that the market equilibrium will be shifted from E_A^7 to E_A^{10}, which is also where the equilibrium for the Dominant is (E_D^{10}). The net price received by the Dominant at the quantity of Q_D^{10} amounts to level B, constituting to a producer surplus of the area BCH, which is larger than the previous size of $P^7E_D^7H$. The increase in the quantity traded also improves the well-being of the collective (area $IE_A^{10}G$ versus area IE_A^7H).

THE OPTIMAL TACTICS MIX

The analyses above show some of the possibilities of the fencing and fostering strategies that may be deployed by the parties involved. When cost considerations are included, strategies that look profitable at first may no longer be beneficial. Yet the cost that matters to the individual is the cost that is attributed to him or her, which may not coincide with the aggregate or social level of cost of his or her actions. When a proposition is deemed as the best option as evaluated on benefit and cost attributed to him or her, an individual may pursue it, even if that brings the collective to a worse-off state.

Whether as a buyer or a seller, the Dominant chooses how and by how much to fence as well as to foster competition. Although pursuing both may have efficiency ramifications on each other due to backfiring, the underlying decision calculus within the rationality model remains the same: to choose the strategy combination that gives him the maximum level of expected net benefit.

What would characterize that level or indeed the optimal allocation of resources among the various strategic options (i.e., consumption, fencing, and fostering)? Applying the same logic on the choice over the level of fencing spending as depicted in figure 11.4 (if the marginal rates of net return of the options are not equal), an individual could raise the total net return simply by allocating resources from the option that gives the lower return to the higher-yielding one. This implies that the optimum is attained when the rates of return of the various options are equal.

Besides the preferences of the parties involved, the outcomes are also subject to the values of the various parameters embedded in the illustrations: for instance, a fencing initiative becoming less effective based on the availability of some new technologies or the discoveries of new trading routes that lower the cost of the Outsider to do business with the Subordinate, resulting in a larger allocation effect or a less significant blocking effect on other buyers, or a combination of both. Expiring patents, which in effect are equivalent to curtailing the fencing capability of the patent holder, very often suggest a change of strategy for the holder from fencing to fostering competition. To develop a model to derive the optimum strategy and illustrate the effects of such changes in the underlying parameters, we are going to modify the neoclassical model by integrating the levels of spending on fencing and fostering competition into it.

12

Expanding the Neoclassical Model

This chapter will further demonstrate how the asymmetric preference on competition intensity and the associated cost consideration and implications can be incorporated into the neoclassical model. The key components will be discussed first, to be followed by an exploration on how to integrate them into the consumer theory and the theories on market structures.

THE COMPONENTS

Total Price

Prices in the neoclassical model are typically taken to mean only the market price of a good. However, one usually has to incur other costs when acquiring a good, which could be search costs, negotiation costs, transport costs, and the like. Those costs may or may not vary in proportion to the quantity of the good that an individual is buying. If one's intended purchase volume, for instance, is not more than what he or she has already located in the market, then he or she no longer has to source for more units. The search costs will stay the same. Transport cost, in contrast, is more likely to change with the size of one's purchase, apart from other factors like shipping distance and mode of transport. Such "extra" costs, typically taken as transaction costs, while only incidental to the transactions, do form part of the total price that one is paying and hence may alter one's purchase decisions accordingly.

If one is to interfere with others' behavior, he or she may alter the total price that he himself or she herself is paying or others are paying. To do that, he or she may try to manipulate the exchange price directly, or take the transaction cost channel by altering the transaction costs that others may have to bear. That is to say, spending on fencing or fostering competition could work not only via the market or exchange price but also by means of transaction costs.

For instance, a subway operator might have discretion over which buildings and shopping malls a subway station being planned will connect to. The operator in effect has significant discretionary power over future passenger flows in the neighborhood and hence the total prices that the passersby are going to pay for accessing the various connected and hence the unconnected (or to be more exact, the more connected and the less connected) buildings and malls in the future. With a larger flow, it is more likely that the corresponding commercial or retail properties will become more valuable.

Realizing he or she has that power, the operator could manipulate the traffic flow and hence the competition intensity differentials among the property owners in the area to his or her benefit. The potential additional revenue that the subway operator collects from exercising that power could subsidize or lower the cost for building the station or, if control against corruption is lax, benefit the staff of the operator in control of that discretionary power personally.

Budget Constraint

Spending on fencing or fostering competition evidently consumes one's resources and hence shall be accounted for by the budget constraint as well. As such, one's budget constraint is composed not only of the direct costs of purchases and transaction costs, which together form the total purchase consideration, but also of the spending on fencing and fostering competition. Given that the spending to alter the competition intensity could be deployed for making purchases instead, an individual's decision to divert resources to those strategies must be based on the expectation that doing so will improve one's overall utility.

Relative Coercive Efficiency

Since the coercive capabilities of different individuals in fencing and fostering competition intensity may not be the same, the net effect and hence the return for each individual's strategies will depend on the relative coercive capabilities or the differentials in the quality or productivity of the strategies pursued by the individuals involved. To form an expectation of the return of one's strategies, it is assumed that each individual has a subjective conversion matrix in mind that translates his or her fencing and fostering strategies into expected returns, taking into account the anticipated strategies of others.[45]

Evidently, one's subjective assessment on his or her coercive capability and that of others may not coincide with the actual. To have a measure on the actual outcomes, we assume that there is an aggregate or social conversion matrix that converts the strategies adopted by the players into actual net outcomes in terms of the distribution of the goods and associated prices that each is going to pay. The social conversion matrix reveals, after taking into account what each and every one has pursued, what each individual gets and at what total price.

How close or how far one's subjective conversion matrix matches with the actual outcomes depends on factors like the individual's knowledge on the social aggregation matrix and information on the strategies to be pursued by other parties. To avoid shouldering loss due to such information discrepancies, each individual will try to align his or her subjective conversion matrix with that of the social one. If obtaining information is not costly and the information obtained is free from deceptive distortions, the individual and the social ones will coincide.

---

45 This is similar to a person making success rate projections when contemplating what to do, a marketing team estimating extra sales that could be generated when drafting a promotion campaign proposal, or a strike unit leader evaluating the pros and cons of different tactical moves when formulating a combat plan.

The Optimum

The typical neoclassical model for the consumer choice problem focuses on the good that a utility-maximizing individual wants to consume, in accordance with his or her own preference set and budget constraint. The individual continues consuming the good until the additional utility or value that the next unit of the good is expected to bring (i.e., marginal utility) is less than the corresponding cost of acquiring it (i.e., marginal cost). Here, he or she will stop consuming or reduce the quantity consumed in order to avoid bearing the negative utility or the loss. The optimum is attained when marginal utility equals marginal cost.

EXPANDING THE MODEL

With the above components, we could incorporate the fencing and fostering propositions into the neoclassical model. To do that, we could substitute the quantity of the good that is taken as the decision variable in the typical neoclassical utility-maximization problem with the levels of spending to fence and foster competition.[46] The quantity of the good that one gets becomes a function of one's spending on the two strategies, in accordance with his or her subjective and the social conversion matrices (with the former for formulating his or her own strategies and the latter for converting one's strategies into actual quantities that are to be acquired and the prices to be paid after aggregating the effects of the strategies of all parties involved). With negligible information costs and undistorted information, such that the individual's subjective conversion matrices align with the social one, the function can be simplified by substituting the subjective conversion matrix with the social one. As such, we have a modified utility function not taking the quantity of the good but rather the levels of spending on the two strategic strands as the decision variables.

As for the budget constraint, since spending on fencing or fostering competition intensity also consumes resources, the constraint (which is

---

46 An alternative is to incorporate the levels of spending on fencing and fostering competition into an expenditure-minimization model.

the aggregate of all outlays[47]) is expanded to include the respective outlays on pursuing those two strategies. As previously mentioned, a utility-maximizing individual will divert resources from the lower-yielding strategy to the higher one in order to improve his or her total utility or total return. At the optimum, the marginal utilities of all strategies are equal, and the individual will find no more swapping opportunities available that are expected to improve his or her total utility. Applying that to the expanded model (or maximizing utility on the modified utility function against the expanded budget constraint) gives an optimum where the marginal utility from fencing equals that from fostering. As such, we have the optimal levels of spending on fencing and fostering competition—and hence the optimal or utility-maximizing quantity of the good that is to be acquired and how it is to be acquired. By aggregating the individual choices on the social conversion matrix, we will obtain the corresponding distribution of the good and the associated price that each is going to pay.

APPLYING TO THE FIRM

As for the firm, we can integrate the model into the profit-maximization problem based on the same logic. For each factor input like labor and capital, instead of acquiring it directly from the market, the firm will deploy fencing or fostering strategies that are most profitable to it. Optimum is reached when the expected marginal returns of fencing competition and fostering competition across the different factors of production are equal.

Market Structure: Continuum or Discrete

In the expanded model, to alter competition intensity to one's benefit has been the main focus. In comparison, in the neoclassical model competition intensities are represented by the four types of market structure. The most intense form of competition—namely, perfect competition—occurs under the stylized setting where there are numerous sellers in the market over which no single party has any influence on the outcome. The worst form of competition (or the lack of it) is monopoly, where there is only one seller

---

47 It is assumed that all is spent on purchasing.

(or one buyer in the case of monopsony). Other market structures in between the two extremes are modeled under different behavior assumptions or represented by response functions that are specified on a case-by-case basis, with the two more commonly cited types being monopolistic competition and oligopoly. Regardless of the type of market structure one is in, the definitive parameter lies in the number of players.

Other than focusing on the number of firms, the market structures are assumed to be discrete under the neoclassical treatment, where each market structure is independent from each other. There is no transition (or no theoretical account of the transitions) from one type of market structure to another. The market structures remain the same. Competition intensity, as represented by the type of market structure, is neither a choice variable nor an end result but a given parameter. That is to say, the market structure is the starting point of study and is assumed to stay unchanged.

In the earlier discussion on the availability of alternatives, it is pointed out that the number of competing players in the market is one of the factors determining the intensity and outcomes of competition. This is premised on the idea that the more alternatives that are available, the more likely an individual is able to find a better offer. Put differently, the more players there are in the market, the more *statistically* likely that competition intensity is higher. Yet this is only a statistical phenomenon, and there is no theoretical link between the number of players and competition intensity. Having "numerous" players in the market is neither a sufficient nor a necessary condition for intense competition.

Under the expanded model, what interests an individual most is engineering the levels of competition intensity in the associated markets such that his or her benefit or utility is maximized. He or she may fence or foster competition in the respective markets by doing so. Since the different means available to him or her for the purpose carry different cost-and-benefit implications, he or she has to decide on the best-yielding strategy when developing his or her competition intensity strategy.

Although the numbers of players on his or her side and the counter-party's side do matter, those are only some of the factors determining the aggregate competition intensity. The capability of the players (whether a few or just one) in tempering the effectiveness of or his her fencing and fostering campaigns may have an even greater impact. Factors like this make the number of firms not the definitive parameter in classifying the intensity of competition or the type of market structure, as is the case in mainstream microeconomics. More importantly, from the perspective of the expanded model, there are no different types of market structure but only markets of different competition intensities. Moreover, competition intensity may be changed by the individuals' strategies to fence or foster competition. As a result, the walls under the neoclassical model separating the types of market structure and making them discrete are dissolved. Market structures are on a continuum instead.

Market Structures Reinterpreted

Given the preceding, how would the models on the four types of market structures be changed when the expanded model is applied to them? Under what conditions would the expanded model mimic the settings of those four types of market structure?

Perfect Competition

In the neoclassical "perfect competition" setting, the optimum condition is where the marginal utility of Good X equals its price in a single-good case, the marginal utility of Good X normalized by price of Good X equals the marginal utility of Good Y normalized by the price of Good Y in a two-good case, or the marginal utilities of all goods (each normalized by its own price) are equal in a multigood case, with all being spent on making the purchases directly.

Applying that to the expanded model implies that no party makes any spending to fence or foster competition. Within the rationality postulate, that will be the case only when the net returns from the two strategies are always inferior to those gained from making the purchases directly.[48] Put

---

48 Purchasing a good makes it not available to other parties as long as that good is a private good. This implies that purchasing can be viewed as a way to fence out competition or a means of fencing spending.

differently, this means the perfect competition scenario is replicated in the modified model when fencing and fostering are always futile. This, in fact, echoes the typical assumption in the perfect competition setting where a price taker is always powerless in influencing the market price, so that fencing and fostering strategies always result in loss.

The key distinction is that in the typical perfect competition model, there are numerous sellers, whereas in the expanded model, the number of sellers is not the definitive factor. What matters in the latter case is that each individual is unable to achieve any gain from pursuing fencing or fostering strategies.[49]

In other words, in the replicated perfect competition setting, we only have players finding it not worthwhile either to fence or to foster competition, but we cannot be sure if there are "numerous" players in the market. There may be just a few players competing fiercely against one another. If we want to have numerous sellers and for that to remain so, as assumed in the neoclassical model, we need to further assume that the initial market is populated as such (i.e., with numerous sellers) and that there are no changes that will destabilize their cost-and-benefit calculi, where some will find it beneficial to fence or foster competition. That is, each seller or buyer will continue to find it not worthwhile to pursue propositions to fence or foster competition.

Monopoly

The case of extreme market power in the neoclassical tradition is represented by "monopoly," where there is only one seller in the market. That is a logical deduction given the prime importance of the number of players in the neoclassical tradition.

To have only one seller in a market within the expanded model, other than making the initial assumption that the market is colonized by one seller only, we need to assume as well that propositions to compete with

---

49 A high number of sellers may be a factor that leads to such a situation, but there could be other factors of the same effect as well. We shall discuss that in more detail in the following chapter.

the dominant incumbent are always not pursued. Under the expanded model, this happens when, for any player considering entry into the market, the proposition to fight against the incumbent is always inferior and hence not taken. That, in turn, may be a result of the supremacy of the incumbent in fighting against any challenge, such that it always pays for that incumbent to fence off competition,[50] not only against potential entrants but also against any efforts by its customers to open the market to potential entrants. On such cost-and-benefit calculi, the market will have only one seller, giving us a monopoly. Similar to the perfect competition case, for the monopoly to be sustainable, it is also assumed that there are no changes to the underlying cost-and-benefit calculi of all players, incumbent or prospective, that will incentivize transformations of the market structure.

Monopolistic Competition and Oligopoly

Different models have been put forward to stylize the remaining two types of market structure, namely "monopolistic competition" and "oligopoly," particularly for the latter category.[51] Although the numbers of sellers in the two types of market structures are different, the sellers in both settings do not command much room to raise prices without having to suffer significant loss of demand for their goods—even in the case of oligopoly, where the players are supposed to enjoy noticeable market power.[52]

To represent those two types of market structure in the expanded model, the corresponding assumptions on the initial numbers of sellers in the market are made in accordance with the respective neoclassical models (i.e., "a lot" in the case of monopolistic competition and "a few" in oligopolies). The leeway on prices or the extent of market power could be represented in the expanded model by the situation where the seller, whether in monopolistic competition or oligopoly, is able to profit from engaging in initiatives to fence or foster competition, but the gain dries up and the

---

50 Citing some common "causes," this may be due to natural monopoly or legal barriers.

51 One can refer to any intermediate-level microeconomics textbook for a brief discussion on these models.

52 For instance, under the kinked demand curve model, an oligopolist may have to bear significant drops in quantity demanded when raising the selling price.

propositions will turn into loss-making ventures when the spending on those propositions surpasses a certain level. How far that level is from the seller's initial position or how big the gain is from pursuing those propositions can be taken as a measure of a seller's market power. That is, a seller with larger market power is represented by a larger limit such that there is more room for spending on fencing or fostering competition before that becomes loss making on a marginal basis. Likewise, a less powerful seller reaches the limit with only some small additional spending on those strategies.

Within the above framework, there is no logical certainty on the relationships between the number of sellers in the market and the size of the limit. The limit for a seller under the monopolistic competition setting does not have to be smaller than that for an oligopolist. Oligopolies in a highly competitive industry may not have any leeway on prices, while a grocery stall in a small town might have some flexibility. Assuming that the sizes of the two markets are the same, we only know that it is more likely for an oligopolist to have a higher market share and revenue than a monopolistic competitive seller.

With a significantly higher market share and hence higher revenue, it is again merely statistically more likely for the oligopolist to have a larger limit than a seller operating under monopolistic competition conditions. That is neither a sufficient condition nor a theoretical requirement. It is quite possible for a seller in a monopolistic competition to have a higher limit than an oligopolist as classified on their shares of a market. Factors like price transparency and price consciousness need to be taken into account as well.

*   *   *

The above illustrates how the four types of market structure—assumed to be discrete under mainstream neoclassical microeconomics—can be replicated in the expanded model. Markets of different competition intensities can be represented under a unified framework and no longer need to be taken as discrete. Instead, they exist on a continuum. Individuals or firms may pursue propositions to alter the competition intensity of a market to their benefit. As we shall see in more detail in the following chapters, transformations, particularly in the context of political economy and not only the theories of the firm, from one type to another (or the lack thereof) can also be accounted for by the expanded model.

13

Choice, Competition, and
Market Democracy

Evidently, analysis on competition dynamics or the choice mechanism is not limited to consumer theory and market structures. Institutional arrangements, especially market democracy, are also closely related topics. Market economy and democracy are now generally taken as the preferred institutional mechanism for organizing economic and political activities of a society, particularly after the failure of the communist model. It is also maintained that the adoption of either would lead to that of the other, and the adoption of both would mutually enhance their effectiveness and put the society on a more solid footing for continued progress. Both systems are premised on individual freedom and choice. As such, the neoclassical model can be taken as the stylized representation, especially for the market economy.

Nonetheless, the robustness of the twin is not uncontested, especially in the face of some counterexamples that cannot be readily discredited. In China, for instance, even after the market model was adopted in a large part of its economy with considerable success, the Communist Party's monopoly in the political arena remains firmly in grip, if not more so, putting in doubt the argument that the adoption of one leads to another. Prolonged instabilities and failures to bring social and economic improvements to the mass public in some countries that have adopted both market economy and democracy, like some African and Middle East nations, suggest that there may be missing pieces in the argument that adopting both brings prosperity to the whole community.

Those anomalies cannot be accounted for by the neoclassical model. This chapter applies the expanded model to address those issues, with the focus on the choice mechanism. We shall see how that mechanism can bring forth the robust version of the twin and hence how to handicap the effectiveness of that twin.

THE ROBUST MODEL

Two Facets of Individual Choice

The robustness of both market economy and democracy is largely built upon the common thesis of choice, two facets of which are of particular importance. The first is "self-determination in decision making," meaning that it is the individual who determines for himself or herself what propositions he or she is to pursue or accept. Even if the choice is made by others for him or her, it is only after his or her consent is obtained, directly or indirectly, deemed or actual. In fact, arrangements as to who makes the choice are one of the key distinctions between market democracy and other institutional settings like an authoritarian regime or a communist country. In a market economy, it is the consumer who decides what to buy for himself or herself, while in a communist planned model, it is the bureaucracy that decides what each citizen gets, typically through a rationing system.

Self-determination in choice also includes deciding on what grounds a consumer bases his or her preference or choice, knowingly or subconsciously. For instance, a student may shop for a personal computer based on criteria like application performance and graphical quality, while the purchasing department of a multinational group may do so based on system compatibility and after-sales services. Similarly, individuals may decide what to do for a living based on considerations and projections they regard as important or relevant. One may take on an employment offer that has the highest monetary pay, or one of mediocre earnings but with what one perceives as significant nonmonetary value. One could also vote for any presidential candidate he or she thinks possesses the attributes he or she regards as significant for running the country, including perceived problem-solving capabilities, public-speaking skills, affinity factors, and the like.

The second facet of choice is the appropriation of the benefit and the cost of a proposition to the parties concerned, such that there is no incomplete or mistaken matching between the pursuits of an individual and the consent of the parties. One chooses the option that entails the best expected net benefit to himself or herself. The effects on others from that option are reciprocated back to him or her, which may take the form of support if others benefit from that pursuit and prefer it to be taken, demands for compensation if they suffer from it, or merely inaction.[53] Such appropriation thereby embeds the consent or interests of other parties back into the cost-and-benefit calculus of the individual who pursues the proposition. In other words, failure in appropriation may twist the concerned parties' cost-and-benefit matrices and distort the deployment of resources accordingly. Appropriation is therefore imperative in establishing the incentive structure for the pursuit of a proposition.

Linking Individual and Social

Since propositions made by an individual as to what and how to pursue are judged by the other parties involved, the outcome of a pursuit will be decided by how well received it is by the rest. For instance, how many others would like to buy what one puts up for sale, and how much each is willing to pay for it? Or how many voters would cast their votes for the proposal introduced by a political group? As long as an individual can secure an audience or support of a size deemed sufficient, as measured against the applicable purposes and standards, one's proposition may be accepted. A choice mechanism structured as above when adopted as the organizing theme for a society intertwines the interests of all parties of the collective, despite choices being made on the individual level.[54]

---

53 Whether inaction carries an affirmative or negative connotation needs to be related to factors like applicable laws and social customs as well.

54 This is supported by theoretical undertakings such as the Walrasian model, which states that self-interest activities will bring individuals and the collective to an equilibrium point that coincides with the optimum, or best possible state.

Betterment of the Best

Given that under the neoclassical model a proposition is accepted only on the voluntary choice of the other parties involved, a proposition being accepted implies that it is regarded by the choice makers as the best among the options available, putting the individuals and the community in the best possible state, the optimum. If a new choice emerges and is regarded as even better, the incumbent will be abandoned. Subject to its being justified on a net benefit basis, such an incentive structure motivates community members to bring up better choices.

Moreover, if the cost for alternatives to emerge is lower or the benefit from which is higher in a collective, it is more likely that more options would be made available. It is also more likely for any individual to get an alternative that fits his or her preferences more closely or even exceeds his or her expectations, or the more likely betterments over the already chosen become available.

With self-determination, along with the appropriate definition and enforcement of benefit and cost, individuals and the collective are incentivized to continuously search for betterments. The more options that can be made available (or the more intense the competition is), the more likely individuals are able to choose offers that are better than the current ones. Since the previously chosen one represents the best available at the time when it was chosen, the emergence of a better alternative implies betterment of the best, both individually and collectively. From a dynamic perspective, the collective is focused on continued searches for betterments.

Market democracy, with the appropriate definition and enforcement of property and political rights, resembles the above setting most closely. The dynamics of both hinge on giving individuals the freedoms to choose, which moves individuals and the collective to their best possible state, and links individual and social interests together. The appeal of the twin spans not as much on the abilities to mobilize resources (as an authoritarian regime could also achieve that and may even be more effective in doing so in some cases) but more on the notion that the mechanism is based on individual choice on the one hand and could attain the interests of the collective on the other hand.

INFALLIBLE?

The above outlines how the choice mechanism could bring out the robust version of market economy and democracy. Yet as argued earlier, after allowing for the possibility of inflicting damage on others, the robustness of the choice mechanism and the neoclassical model is compromised. Strong incumbents may pursue propositions to fence or foster competition in the corresponding markets to benefit themselves, regardless of the type of system they are in.

Mutually Reinforcing?

As mentioned, market economy and democracy both operate on the individual choice premise. Adopting them both not only brings compatible results but also reinforces each other. For instance, decentralization of control on economic resources in a market economy would lessen the likelihood of a dictatorship or uncontested concentration of power in politics and strengthen the foothold of a democracy.[55] We have also pointed out that under the expanded model, the threat of being displaced could keep the incumbent ruling faction from implementing policies detrimental to the economic interests of the subjects with the displacement power, which could be the mass in cases of a majority democracy, further supporting the thesis that the two are mutually reinforcing.

However, is it inevitable that the adoption of either market economy or democracy leads to the adoption of the other? Parties who have the right to make a choice in one arena are incentivized to ensure that a system that most protects their interests is also in place in other arenas. If the parties are able to exercise voluntary choice in a market economy profitably, it is natural for them to find ways to protect that capacity on, say, the political side. Democracy, in which economic interests typically take a high priority,

---

55 M. Friedman, *Capitalism and Freedom* (Chicago: The University of Chicago Press, 1982), 8–9.

could keep a ruling party from infringing the rights of the public and is generally regarded as an institutional arrangement capable of achieving that. Similarly, those who find their political interests being well served in a democracy would also endeavor to have an economic system that best protects their political rights. The market system, where individuals with political power can usually exercise their economic choice to their benefit, is commonly rendered as the economic counterpart or complement to democracy.

Always Passive?

Effective choice, however, is not always exercisable. A choice within a choice domain where only one option is allowed, which probably is the incumbent offer, can hardly be taken as meaningful. To have meaningful choices, the choice domain needs to be open and competitive. Yet that may imply displacements of incumbents, such as a long-established and highly profitable beverage being outcompeted by a new drink, a recording medium format forced out of favor by consumers looking for a more versatile alternative, or a ruling party losing a general election. For that to happen, we need each of the parties opting for the new option to have a cost-benefit matrix where sticking with the status quo is no longer the best proposition and the new option becomes the preferred choice.

Unless staying in business or in office is already an inferior option, in which case the incumbent would not continue to engage anyway, one does not expect it to accept defeat without contemplating the launching of countermeasures at all. That is to say, instead of merely choosing between staying put and quitting, as maintained by the neoclassical model, it is also likely, if not more so, for the incumbent to evaluate the options of fencing or fostering competition. It may be more profitable for the incumbent to fence competition by constraining the choice of others or putting counterparties in more disadvantaged competition positions by altering their corresponding cost-and-benefit calculi (by, say, raising their cost of maneuvers or shrinking their profitability of launching challenges). That is, if justified by the corresponding expected net benefits, the incumbent, rather than conceding defeats, may preempt challenges, refuse to leave, or even expel the newly arrived entrants altogether.

In fact, assuming those who lose from competition always refrain from taking fencing or fostering actions that may be profitable but accept losses submissively contradicts the rationality postulate. In contrast, the success of challenges (or the imminent threat of such) made possible in a competitive setting may well push the incumbent to inhibit competition intensity and moves the market from a competitive one to a lesser state.

Disabling Effective Choice

As pointed out earlier, the differentials in the capabilities in fencing or fostering competition among individuals are a key factor in one's decision as to whether to alter the cost-and-benefit matrices of others for one's benefit. The more capable side typically has the upper hand in the deployment, or threat, of fencing or fostering strategies, hence constricting the weak side's effective scope of choice. That may happen even in a market democracy, as the strong side can limit the maneuverability of the weak by means of extensive ownership of physical or intellectual properties, leveraging on its size in the markets to price out buyers' access to alternative sellers or sellers' access to other buyers, or acquiring the challengers to dissolve the competition altogether.

Similarly, in the political arena, a dominant political party may put up formidable obstacles to prevent a democratic system from becoming competitive or make the one already in place nominal in effect. For instance, it may sweep out challenges by prosecuting opponents or by imposing costly or practically unattainable requirements for an alternative choice to be presented to voters. More directly, a dominant political faction unseated in an election may stage a postelection military clampdown or coup.

From a cross-model perspective, the economic dominants might protect and enhance their interests by extending their reach to the political camp by means of forming a dominant politico-economic ruling complex. Candidates who are not allegiances of the dominant complex may be made unable to gather the resources to stage a campaign to run for office. In cases with only one major party strong enough to form and run a government, the choice mechanism as the disciplinary force to protect and further the interests of the individual subjects can hardly be manifest.

We can see that even in a market economy, especially when there are only a very few factions that command extensive control on economic resources, the robustness of the choice mechanism could be seriously impaired. Those with the strong bargaining power can squeeze out gains from the lesser, impose a choice of negatives on them, or simply keep them out of the game. The disadvantaged may be locked in the lesser status, even if sustained economic growth and rising employment levels are happening on the aggregate level.[56] Such end results resemble more of an authoritarian regime than that under a stylized market democracy.

By the same token, on the choice over system type, the factions that have the capability to decide which type of system to be adopted will prefer the type that is more capable of securing or furthering their interests. While the choice might be market democracy per se, it could also be an authoritarian regime having adopted a market economy, or a market-democracy combo with the choice mechanism twisted decisively to their advantage. Whatever the choice, the strong side may simply manipulate competition intensity to their advantage and disable the effective choice of the mass, even though the choice mechanism may still be of the market-democracy type. The twin model of market democracy may not bring the collective to the social ideal as stipulated by the neoclassical model.

One After Another?

By the same rationale, the adoption of either the market mechanism or democracy may not lead to the adoption of the other. Having one in place does not suggest that the other will be adopted soon. In cases where only one or a very few players are dominant in one arena, even if major changes are to be made to a system, it is likely that the dominant players would (if within their capacity and to their benefit) ensure that their positions

---

56 M. Sharma et al., "Rising Inequality with High Growth and Falling Poverty," *An Eye on East Asia and Pacific, World Bank* (Washington, DC: World Bank, 2011), no. 9, 1–6.

remain secure in the new landscape. It is therefore likely that they would push for or maintain an antichoice mechanism in the other arena.

A noticeable example of this is the case of China, where the market economy model is being implemented to supersede the planned model. Inefficiencies in the economy are being squeezed out, and huge growth momentum has been unleashed. The people are given more freedom of choice in daily life, particularly in economic areas. However, the whole reform series has been implemented within the larger context of upholding the dominance of the Communist Party in the reformed system. No other entity could, or is expected to be able to, challenge the dominance of the party, and the reforms have hardly resulted in undermining the political control of the Communist Party. Rather, its dominance has been merely migrated to the new system.

CHANGES IN COMPETITION INTENSITY

Whether or not a choice mechanism is competitive largely depends on the distribution of fencing and fostering capabilities in the collective. A robust choice mechanism is typically premised on a more even distribution in those capabilities. Changes in competition intensity therefore may originate from corresponding changes in the distribution of those capabilities. For instance, a transformation from a repressive model to a more competitive one may be a consequence of the accumulation of wealth or resources by the nonincumbents to the extent that is eventually sufficient to force changes.

Another possible cause, typically involving redistributions within a short horizon, is that the poorer subjects are pushed to a life-and-death situation and pose meltdown risks to the system, stretching the incumbent party's capability to the limit in sustaining its position (like the Paris mobs during the French Revolution). Changes could also be precipitated by a collapsing incumbent or political framework, like the collapse of the czarist throne in the run-up to the Russian Revolution. The incumbents in both examples, particularly in the czarist case, faced very disadvantaged resource constraints as well as discontented citizenry and military, rendering them powerless to fence off the revolts and unrests, and giving the challengers the chance to swiftly build up their dominance.

Besides those possibilities, a move to a more even distribution could also be a result of the incumbent factions becoming rivals and such rivalry turning into competition for the support of the lesser subjects, benefiting the latter consequentially. An example would be the early phase of the individual revolution where the capitalists bid for labor inputs as part of their larger competition in the product markets—where the workers, especially those with skills in short supply, could obtain better pay more readily as a result of the capitalists' rivalries. Competition intensity in the labor markets increases as a result of the competition among the capitalists in the product markets. The workers become better off gradually, enabling them to rally for a more competitive political system to represent and protect their interests.

THE PROBLEM OF THE DOMINANT

While the two models of market economy and democracy could bring benefit to all, the adoption of either does not necessarily lead to the adoption of the other, nor is the adoption of either one or both always beneficial to all. There are plenty of possibilities. The dominant player may remain dominant or become even more so based on the adoption of any one or both by capitalizing on the higher systemic productivity and at the same time manipulating the system workings to an advantage by pursuit of corresponding strategies to fence or foster competition. The disadvantaged may as a result continue to remain disadvantaged, or even more so.

The actual choices made by the individuals and the results from the interactions of those choices depend on the respective cost-and-benefit calculi, and the distribution of those capabilities. That is, even if either one or both models are adopted by some explicit efforts, it is likely not for protecting and facilitating the exercising of freedoms or rights of individuals or for any other ideological grounds, but merely because the adopted model happens to be the most beneficial option. Hence, when evaluating the pros and cons of the market-democracy twin as a theoretical construct or as a mechanism to be adopted (or any institutional arrangements to that effect), we must not ignore the power of the dominant, which may leverage its dominance to benefit at the expense of others and thereby compromise the effectiveness of the choice mechanism.

To further analyze the problem of the dominant, we are going to revisit the problem of how to discipline the state in the next chapter. The setting of the analysis will be pushed to the extreme—that on one hand, there is only one dominant entity in the collective (i.e., the state), and on the other hand, it is assigned the task of pursuing the interests of the subjects.

14

Dilemma of the State

Whether for a market democracy or any type of collective other than anarchy, questions of what a state *is* and what a state *should be* are fundamental to political economic studies. As to the question of what a state is, one basic requirement is that it can function effectively, or it is capable of enforcing its rule in the domain over which it claims to have jurisdiction. Alternatively speaking, the effectiveness of a state is in doubt when it is unable to enforce its rule to the extent it claims it can.

Nevertheless, for a state to have effective rule, it needs to be not only in the state's interests to enforce its rule, but also in the interests of the subjects to comply with the state's rule. Compliance by the latter may be a result of direct benefit from doing so or to avoid suffering a larger pain. A key element here is that the state is the most powerful and efficient coercive entity in the collective, such that it is always prohibitively costly for the rest to fight against it, making compliance the subjects' preferred choice. Without that capability, the state is more inclined toward (if not resorting to) offering benefits to subjects as its means to enforce its rule. However, on such a path the subjects may render that defying the state's rule, or even toppling it, is within their reach and to their benefit, putting the stability of the administration in jeopardy.

The above does not necessarily mean that the state must be the monopoly of coercive power in the domain. There could be other parties that are coercively abled. Local governments in a feudal society or a federal union are examples of peripheral units in legitimate possession of coercive forces, while organized gangs are the illegitimate ones. The state just needs to be the strongest, though the larger the differential in relative coercive capabilities the state commands,[57] the less likely its rule will be challenged.

Given that it is the strongest entity, no one is able to pose a credible challenge to the rule of the state. This also means that no party can become a meaningful threat to discipline it. However, without any effective disciplinary force in place, how could it be sure that the state will, say, uphold the interests of the subjects? Yet if there are factions strong enough to discipline the state, this means it is no longer the strongest, in turn putting its ability to rule (if not the stability of the community as well) in doubt. The contradictory requirements of the state being the strongest and yet disciplinable is in essence the dilemma of the state.

A SELF-INTEREST STATE

The dilemma is premised on two assumptions: the first on the nature of the state and the second on what the state is to do. For the first assumption, as depicted earlier, it is assumed that the state is a self-interest entity and not run by persons of some compassionate attributes, interpreted as caring about the interests of others first, if not solely. This assumption is made because with such compassionate persons in office, the interests of the subjects would be upheld simply because of the virtues of the entrusted. Here, the question of what type of institutional arrangements minimizes the chance of having a malignant administration becomes irrelevant.

Moreover, how can we be sure that there are such compassionate or altruistic persons in the community? Even if we do have such altruistic individuals in a collective, how could we be sure that they are chosen to run the state with its supreme power? Most difficult of all, how could we be sure that the chosen altruistic would remain altruistic after being entrusted with the power? Does that mean we should extend the assumption

---

57 It is also not a must for the state to maintain the coercive capability directly. The state only needs to have command of the use of force when needed, or even for a definite period of time or for some specific purpose. That is, this "force" may not always need to be a full-scale conventional military force but could merely consist of mercenaries or allies willing to fight for or alongside it.

to every individual chosen for office or assume that every individual in the collective is altruistic and will remain so? That is evidently only assuming the problem away. With no evil, we may not need a state at all.

As such, we are not making the assumption that the state is run by altruistic persons or, more directly, that the state is intrinsically good and takes care of subjects' interests by nature. Instead, it is assumed that the state is like any other party in the collective, meaning that it is a self-interest entity that cares about (and only about) pursuing its own interests. The well-being of the subjects matters, if at all, only as one of the factors in a state's cost-and-benefit calculus.[58]

THE ROLE OF THE STATE

The preceding indeed gives a basic answer to the question of what a state is: the state is the strongest entity that pursues its self-interest. To that end, the dilemma becomes how to discipline a self-interest state that is the strongest in the collective or the most capable of enforcing its will. So we need to further question what a state should be disciplined to do, or what constitutes an ideal state. This is because, without the need to take on any presupposed role, we are left with the question of what the state does with its power to the citizenry, which is largely a prediction issue and not one of political philosophy. We would then be focusing only on what *would* happen, not what *should* happen, and we would have no dilemma at all. The dilemma of the state falls between what the state *is* and what the state *should be*, or the nature and capability of the state versus its presupposed role.

The Ideal Political State

This brings us to the second assumption, which is focused on the role of the state or what the state is supposed to do. There are generally two trajectories of arguments regarding the role of the state. The first stems

---

58 Making the assumption that the state is not compassionate could also help us avoid falling prey to the fallacy where the new system is always virtuous and the previous one always evil. For instance, Marx assumed that the comrades of the communist state would take good care of all and make everyone happy, suggesting that it was safe and right to surrender all rights and freedoms to the Communist Party.

primarily from the debate on political philosophy surrounding what constitutes an ideal state, while the second is about the economic role of the state, particularly in terms of resolving the failures of the market system.

From the political philosophy's perspective, the debate on the ideal state primarily is on how the state carries out the will of the subjects, whether collectively (e.g., Marxism) or individually (e.g., liberalism). For the latter strand, it is whether it is carried out within the constraint of the laws (e.g., constitutionalism) or not (e.g., anarchy). For political systems of the authoritarian or fascist trait, the general view on those models is negative, which primarily originates from the criticism that the will or the interests of the individuals are secondary to that of the ruler.

In view of the general current inclination of the arguments on the topic, we make the assumption on what an ideal state should do from the political philosophy perspective: that an ideal state is to pursue policies in accordance with the interests of its subjects. This not only goes along with the generally held notion of what a state should be, hence the assumption of the de facto governance principle and evaluation standard for the performance of a state, but also poses probably the most contrasting and opposing stance against the assumption we have made on the nature of the state: that it is a self-interest entity. We require the self-interest state to work for the interests of its subjects.

The Ideal Economic State

That role of the state assumed from the political philosophy side, in fact, is similar to that in economics, which is primarily concerned with rectifying failures of the market system. "Failures" are essentially defined with reference to any deviation of the equilibrium or end state from the social optimum, through which individual interests are best enshrined. The key function of the state is as an alternative provider of "essential" goods, such as some social welfare and judicial services, and administration of the private property rights system. While there has indeed been no prima facie support for the state to be a better alternative, economists (those in support of the argument that the state is a just or impartial party, and those against it) tend to adopt the view that the state should be such an entity, particularly in upholding the interests of the subjects. This echoes the notion of "ideal state" portrayed by political philosophers.

ASCERTAINING AND AGGREGATING INDIVIDUAL INTERESTS

For the state to uphold the interests of its subjects, other than ascertaining individuals' interests, we also need to have some aggregation criteria in place to determine, based on the individuals' interests, what the interests of the collective are. For private goods in a market where each consumer chooses to buy the goods and buy at the prices one wants to, and each seller chooses to sell and sell at prices one chooses to, the aggregation task is performed by the market. For instance, an individual choosing to put up his or her goods for sale in a particular marketplace faces competition from those selling identical or substitutable (wholly or partially) goods in the market, and needs to seek patronage from the same group of potential buyers having access to that marketplace, with each making decisions based on his or her own interests. The market in effect acts as the aggregation medium for the individual-based buying and selling interests of the buyers and the sellers, respectively.

For political systems, classifying in terms of the degree of participation by the members of the collective, we can imagine they range from a pure dictatorship where one decides for all to a full-consent democracy where affirmation is required from every member of the community on every issue. The dictatorial end obviously is plagued with problems of abuse of power, while the full-consent model is likely to be paralyzed by organizational problems on a practical level. Yet the fundamental cause for such complications in political systems largely stems from the bundled nature of political issues.

In this scenario, we each choose, subject to our individual budget constraints, the goods we each like most in a market, but we cannot have a community, at least not yet, where each member chooses a political policy specifically designed and applicable to oneself. That, in fact, closely resembles the public goods problem in economics, as discussed below.

The Problem of Public Goods

In the neoclassical model, for private goods traded in a competitive market, what is best on the individual basis is also the best for the society. Problems arise when dealing with public goods, which are characterized by nonexclusivity in consumption, meaning consumption of such goods by one individual does not prevent or exclude that by others. Common examples of public goods are streetlights and national defense. The provision of street illumination or national protection services to one does not preclude its availability to another, in contrast to the consumption of a private good (like an apple) by one makes it unavailable to others. Such nonexclusivity in consumption also suggests that consumption of public goods by one individual does not require additional goods to be provided for consumption by others.[59]

Nonexclusivity usually leads to the problem of "free riders," or those who benefit from consumption without paying. When consumption is nonexclusive, it is also usually not worth spending to charge the consumers or the users, especially on the usage basis. Not charging separately or even not charging at all may make provision of such goods a loss-making venture.[60] That is, even where the aggregate value exceeds the aggregate provision cost (not counting the charging cost), the good may be not provided due to the high cost of charging. Hence, in such cases where the provision of a certain public good is essential to the well-being of the community but the market "fails" to provide it, it gives the state the grounds to "rectify" the market failures.

---

59 Technically, the social demand curve for public goods, as a result, is obtained by vertically summing up the individuals' demand curves, rather than horizontally as in the case of private goods.

60 Charging could be by indirect means. For example, one could run a restaurant, a kiosk, or the like at a sightseeing point where no access charge is levied. The commercial value of the site is indirectly realized by means of profit from the restaurant or the customer-flow business set up there.

Yet the above state intervention argument is premised on two assumptions, which are both questionable. The first is that, as pointed out, the cost of charging is excluded. If it is not provided by the private market, this may very well be due to the fact that the all-in cost exceeds the total benefit that can be collected. That is, it may not be socially beneficial to supply the goods when all costs are counted. For the state to make it socially beneficial, we need the state to be the more efficient provider than the market, particularly in the task of charging.

The state typically resolves the issue only by getting around it, by leveraging its overwhelming coercive power to fund the provision by collecting payments in the name of taxes or levies. It may not be the more efficient provider at all, and the provision of the goods on the aggregate level may remain a loss-making exercise when all costs are included. It is funded largely by policies deliberately delinking charging and usage.

The second problem relates to the scale of nonexclusivity. There are indeed limits to the scale of nonexclusivity. For instance, there is a limit as to the size of the area that can be illuminated by a given amount of light or protected by a designated size of coercive force. The intensity may also vary in accordance with the corresponding needs of the users in the service area. For instance, some may prefer brighter illumination and for longer hours. Organizers of antique jewelry auctions may require swift and targeted protection, in contrast to a suburban grocery store. Requirements for national defense of a tourist resort island and an oil-producing country are also noticeably different.

After all, as far as one benefits from the consumption of a certain good, one is willing to pay for it. Whether one's consumption of the good excludes the same by others is indeed irrelevant. One only needs to evaluate whether or not its net benefit from that is the best available option. The problem of public goods, in fact, stems less from their nonexclusivity but more from the high cost of charging the users individually and the difficulties in making the provision profitable, which is a commercial matter rather than an intrinsic or systemic issue. That brings us back to the argument made against the first questionable assumption of excluding the charging cost when calculating the total cost.

Take the illumination provided by means of roadside light posts as an example. There may be a certain number of drivers who prefer illuminated roads, while some find using their own headlights to be sufficient. Nonetheless, unlike the choice on whether to turn on the light in a bedroom, we do not have a choice on the street illumination services. Road authorities or administrators have some roads illuminated and some not and, for the illuminated streets, at times and for durations not chosen by the users but in accordance with the policy decisions of the administrators. This is the same whether the roads are publicly or privately owned.

This is largely due to the current applied technologies of road illumination. We cannot have the lights turned on for those preferring such and off for those not wanting them on, especially when both types of drivers are on the same sections of highways at the same time. Even if that is technically feasible, we also need the corresponding charging arrangements in place for those who prefer having the illumination services. To reduce occurrences of traffic accidents due to inadequate illumination, it has become acceptable that the services are provided on a bundled basis, with charges decoupled from usage. The state is either to be the direct service provider or the party responsible for outsourcing and administering the provision contracts on public roads.

With the aid of increasingly advanced measurement, pricing, and other associated transactional technologies, not all of what is currently regarded as in the public goods domain needs to be always provided and charged on a bundled basis. It is well conceivable that, instead of installing streetlights on the highways, illumination services are provided by, say, night goggles or projecting the corresponding road images onto the windscreens or glasses of those drivers who prefer "illumination" services. This is because illumination, after all, is about seeing the images that are visible under the illumination. Projection of those images as such serves the same purpose. Indeed, one could even have options on, say, the brightness of the illumination or the resolution of the images. When such image projection technology becomes available in commercially viable terms, we may no longer need light posts at all.[61] In this case, charging on a usage basis could be arranged and is likely to be so at a reduced cost correspondingly.

Thus, assuming the supply and demand of what are now regarded as public goods can be ascertained and matched on the individual or user level, like a typical private good, and that appropriations of costs and benefits from the social level back to the individual level are viable (thereby unbundling "nonexclusivity" or making it distinguishable on an individual basis[62]), the problem arising from the provision of public goods can be resolved without having them provided by the state. Provision of public goods is not a task that is "intrinsically" or "inevitably" in the domain of the state.

Without the public goods concern, the main issue concerning the dilemma of the state therefore remains how to discipline the strongest entity in the community from abusing its coercive capability but carrying out policies in accordance with the interests of the subjects. That is, we are looking for ways to make pursuing policies aligned with the interests of the subjects in the interest of the state—leveraging, but not abusing, it having the strongest coercive capability.

AS THE PROPERTY RIGHTS AND JUSTICE ADMINISTRATOR

The state is also commonly assigned the role of the administrator of property rights and justice systems, with the former primarily in the economics discipline and the latter politics. For the state to carry out that dual role, it is important that the meanings of "loss" and "wrongs" can be substantiated. Being harmed means one has suffered or that one is being put in a position

---

61 Indeed, imagining that all images could be projected onto, say, a pair of glasses or transmitted to our visual system directly, we may not need illumination services in any place at all.

62 Another route of unbundling that has been put into practice on a large scale involves what is usually grouped under the theme of direct democracy, with referendums being one of the more notable methods. Again, advancements in communications and interaction technologies would accelerate the shift of policy making from the bundled basis to a case-by-case one.

that is worse than before. To validate that claim, one needs to substantiate one's initial state or what one is entitled to, as well as the present situation. A property rights and a justice system that could validate the entitlements and rights, respectively, of all parties in the society are the prerequisites.

However, a property rights system does not have to be a private property rights system as commonly adopted in market democracies. It could be the extreme communist form in which the party owns everything, making it futile and meaningless for the subjects to sue the party to reclaim their "losses." Also, whether the rights as defined by the justice system in place correspond with what one thinks of as "just" and "fair" is another matter. What is more likely is that the incumbent state enacts and enforces a property rights and justice systems where "loss" and "wrong" propositions can be defined accordingly, only for substantiating and sustaining its rule and dominance in the community.

RESOLVING THE DILEMMA

A general case can be built by further examining the dilemma. We have argued that intense competition (or the ready availability of alternatives) can be a strong disciplinary force on a self-interest entity. In the case of a state, that means that the state must be facing enemies or counterforces strong enough to topple its rule or, if the party in charge of the state apparatus is separable from the state as in a competitive democracy, unseat it from the position. Yet to have smooth enforceability of its rule, the state also needs to be the strongest entity in the community, bringing us back to the dilemma of the state.

A way out of the dilemma is that the excess of the state may be constrained by challenges of comparably mighty, or even superior, parties but not by individual subjects. A credible disciplinary force may be formed by means of collusion among the subjects, which emerges when, say, the state pursues policies in breach of its prescribed role of promoting the interests of the citizenry. Under such a setting, we may then have the state to be the strongest on the one hand, thereby ensuring its effectiveness in enforcement, and on the other hand constrained to the pursuits of propositions not contravening but promoting the interests of the subjects.

The question then becomes, how can such a coalition be formed? Within the cost-and-benefit context, we can see that the benefit for the subjects forming such a coalition would stem from forcing the state to tilt its rule or policies more to their advantage or to abandon implementing those policies detrimental to their interests. While we might imagine that such profitable opportunities are often available, we do not see coalitions, especially those of a formidable capability, emerging frequently, particularly in countries without a competitive political system.

What may prevent such coalitions from forming? Given the dominant strength of the state, it is likely that it is the cost of colluding, particularly in the form of punishments, that usually hinders them from forming. Other than the possibility that the poor may simply be unable to afford access to an effective communication network, it could also be that attempts to challenge the state's dominance are uncovered and crushed well before a collusion bloc of a credible size is formed. Parties deemed involved might face stiff punishments as a consequence, as shown by the typical heavy sentences for subversion, especially in countries where the political opposition force is weak.

In contrast, if there are ways to raise the benefit or lower the cost of forming a challenge coalition, or any combination of them, it is more probable that the state's excesses would be restrained. For instance, the availability of Internet connection, particularly due to its dispersed nature, facilitates posting of viewpoints, formation of collective opinions, and organization of protest efforts. The availability of better communications technology or organization efficiency may lead subjects to expect that a credible bloc could be formed within a shorter period of time and that the chance of its being preempted or crushed is lower, in turn making it more likely that the initiative would be put into action.

Anchorages

Apart from advancements in communications technologies to the advantage of the subjects, credible challenge blocs may be formed swiftly from incidents that anchor attention and efforts, thereby rallying resources for the purpose more readily. Changes in staff policies adverse to the interests of the workers may result in strikes, for instance, while policies that jeopardize the livelihood of the public may lead to demonstrations. Invasions by foreign aggressors might help the administration to rally civil support and assemble troops within a short time span. Extensive media reporting of occurrences of large-scale natural disasters may garner widespread attention, as well as quickly summon rescue and relief efforts. Such events or causes have the potential to serve as anchorages on which coalition efforts can be formed swiftly.

The effect of those anchorages might be reinforced further by some prominent or anchorage figures, like Garibaldi and King Emmanuel II as in the case of the unification of Italy, or like Gandhi in the independence movement in India. On such anchorages, collusions may be rallied more readily and efficiently, in effect posing more credible and formidable threats against the incumbent state.

Democracy as an Anchorage-Forming Mechanism

If a community has in place institutionalized arrangements for challenging the incumbent state such that the subjects can organize and put up challenges via well-defined and established channels, the mechanism in effect functions as an anchorage on which challenge efforts can rally. The cost of doing so would be lower in this case, thereby raising the strength of the disciplinary force.

A common example of this is democracy. Instead of staging protests or organizing civil resistance movements, the dissatisfied only need go to the polling stations to cast their votes during elections. The voting mechanism acts as the anchorage for the incumbent opposition forces to rally together, noticeably lowering the cost of assembling forces, even on a national scale.[63] As long as a challenge coalition of the designated

---

63 Other than lowering the cost of organizing the opposition force, having a challenge mechanism explicitly in place or institutionalized also raises the cost for the incumbent to recede or compromise the workings of the system.

size can be anchored in ballot boxes, the incumbent's rule in a general election or its policy as in a referendum would be defeated, disincentivizing the incumbent from pursuing policies that would encroach on the interests of the whole or segments of the community. Such a possibility constitutess an aggregate threat to the incumbent capable of putting its rule in jeopardy.

Point of Change and the Maximum Challenge Capability

From the above, we could envision a point of change beyond which an incumbent state, party, policy, or motion may be brought down, displaced, or defeated by a challenge force of such might. By comparing that point of change with the maximum challenge capability a community could put up, we could have a gauge on whether an incumbent could be brought down at all. The larger the excess the maximum challenge capability has over the point of change, the stronger the disciplinary force on the state would be.

Reciprocally, when a state is more vulnerable to being overthrown, this also implies that its capability to enforce its rule is weaker or the administration is less stable. A government is an unstable one if a coalition of mediocre strength could topple its rule. Similarly, if a credible opposition collusion were to become a coherent and functioning unit in certain territories of the "country," then the rule of incumbent state would be under more sustained and more intense competition pressure to challenge its rule in those territories. Effective rule may as a result be constrained to only other areas in the "country" but not the whole of it, subjecting the community to fracturing tensions.

Evidently, it could also be the case of the other extreme, where the advantage in the coercive capability the incumbent has is so compelling that even the maximum challenge capability, which may be formed by all the rest of the community or (allowing for diseconomies of scale) a specific combination of the members of the collective bearing that capability, is no match against it. The incumbent party is so strong that no challenging party of a sufficient displacement force can be formed. Here, the point of change lies beyond the maximum capability of the challenge. As such, no effective disciplinary force can be imposed on the state.

In sum, for cases where the maximum challenge force lies within the point of change, the incumbent's rule is in the safe zone. This implies that its target would be to prevent the development of a challenge force of a capability higher than the point of change. Its rule would remain secure as long as that is the case.

Tactics to Move the Points

As one may expect, the maximum challenge capability and the point of change are not necessarily fixed. For instance, there are a number of typical tactics that an incumbent state may take to alter them to its advantage. The incumbent may form a coalition with selected factions in the community in order to strengthen its position and to weaken that of the challenge force. That, in effect, is pushing up the required capability to force through a change as well as undermining the challenge capability. Given the typically lower cost of forming coalitions with fewer parties, the incumbent would tend to side with a small number of powerful factions to form a nexus of partnership for the common interests of perpetuating the rule.

Obviously, the choice on the composition of the coalitions (or more generally, the choice on the countertactics to be deployed) depends on not only the distributions of capital and coercive capabilities but also the rules of the political choice mechanism. Is it by military mightiness that the party to be in charge is decided? Or is the political apparatus a vote-based system? In a one-person-one-vote majority-win democracy, the incumbent party may devise a policy mix that benefits a nexus but not all of the electorates, such that a sufficient number of votes would be cast on its side for the continuation of its rule. The state may embark on development initiatives to the benefit of certain targeted segmental interests. It could also involve redistributive measures like asymmetric tax policies in order to secure the support of specific electorates in the citizenry. The incumbent may benefit by way of votes in the ballot boxes and also from other forms, like donations or sponsorships from electorates.

By the same token, rivals may compete for the position by pledging to implement some other mix of policies that benefits the segments of the community that the incumbent is ignoring or by promising better returns for some of the incumbent's existing allegiances. If not for information cost or other forms of asymmetry (so that all parties face the same cost-and-benefit matrices in getting the support of the community members), it is likely that all competing parties would be drawn to the same best strategy and offer the same policy mix.

However, the challengers are handicapped in the competition, as they do not have the existing state apparatus at disposal such that they cannot launch policies during or before the campaign to the benefit of their current or prospective supporters, making standing on their side and fighting against the incumbent a more risky proposition for the supporters. Nonetheless, that may in turn help strike a tone for the challengers with those fringed out by the incumbent, and it endows the former with an advantage in rallying support from the ignored groups.

Other than forming a coalition nexus, the incumbent may also be able to protect its position via other means to undermine the effectiveness of the challenge capability. For instance, to avoid the effectiveness of its strategies being diluted, the state may scale back the size of the domain and focus on a core area where more effective defenses and rule could be enforced. The Roman Empire was first divided into two by Diocletian when the burden of defending and administering the whole empire from the center became too stretching. That paved the eventual relinquishing of the west when the task to defend that half against the barbarian invasions proved to be unbearable.

Alternatively, the incumbent may fence up competitors. For example, within a democracy where the general mechanism is based on a one-person-one-vote system, rival parties may be fenced up if they are barred by means of some prescreening eligibility criteria. Electorates, as a result, may not have a roster of meaningful candidates to pick from. Similarly, the disciplinary force may be made futile, as only a nonpivotal share of the legislature is open for competition so that the incumbent faces no credible displacement threat despite there being an institutionalized voting mechanism.

Interests of All and the Equilibrium Condition
The above outlines some of the tactics that the incumbent state and the challenge force might take to alter the positions of the point of change and the maximum challenge capability. Evidently, each possible tactical mix carries a corresponding cost-and-benefit matrix. The incumbent state would choose the policy mix that is expected to give it the maximum net benefit.[64] We expect that resources would be continuously put in by the incumbent to garner more support, as long as the additional benefit of doing so exceeds the corresponding extra cost, or the marginal benefit is higher than the marginal cost. Similarly, the incumbent would scale back the operation if the marginal cost were higher than the marginal benefit. That is, equilibrium is attained when the two are equal.

Substituting the amount of goods by the number of subjects, we have a gauge on whether it is optimal for the state to work for the interests of the whole community. Simply put, for cases where that equilibrium occurs within the size of the community, it is not worthwhile for the state to seek the support of the whole community, giving a prima facie case for the state not to work for the interests of all. Put differently, in order for a state to work for the interests of the whole community, we need the equilibrium point to be at or beyond the size of the community.

The preceding can be represented by the following charts, which graphically frame the benefit-and-cost calculus of the incumbent state.

---

64 Power built upon an established nexus of supporting factions may, however, be shaken or destabilized by factors like demographic changes or anchorage events that, for instance, precipitate those typically not voting to come out to vote, consequently outvoting the established nexus.

Figure 14.1.

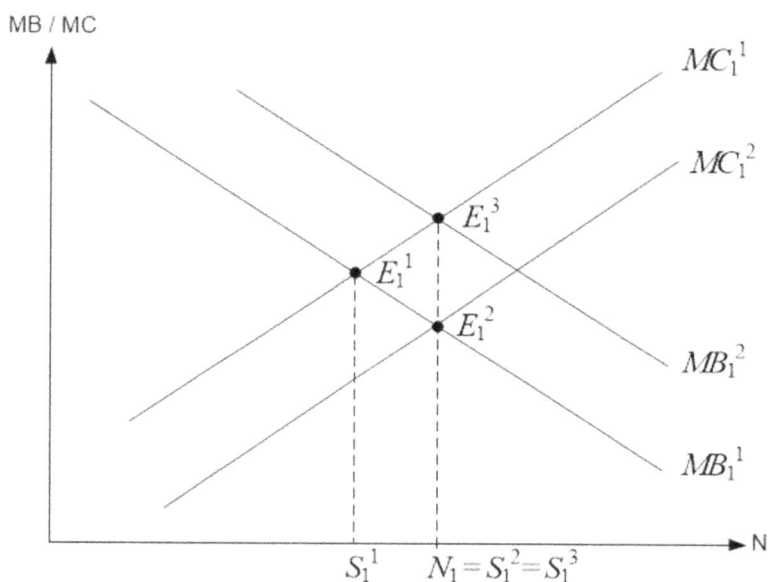

Instead of quantity of goods, the state is posited to adopt the number of citizens as the decision variable for its policy making. As such, the horizontal axis of a typical demand-supply diagram is amended to represent the number of citizens, as in figure 14.1. The benefits for the state to work for the interests of additional citizens are represented by the marginal benefit curves, and the costs of doing such are captured by the marginal cost curves.

Assuming that it gets less and less productive to gain the support of additional subjects, we would have a downward sloping marginal benefit curve. Conversely, if it is increasingly costly to do so, the marginal cost curve is rising. For an arbitrary situation represented by the marginal benefit curve of MB_1^1 and marginal cost curve of MC_1^1, the equality of the two occurs at E_1^1, which is the optimal point for the state. This is because for any number of citizens that lie to the left of the optimum, it is worthwhile for the state to win the support of more citizens, as the marginal benefits associated are higher than the marginal costs. To the right, the contrary is the case, where the marginal costs are higher than the marginal benefits. The S_1^1 level represents the optimal number of subjects whose interests the state is to work for.

Comparing S_1^1 with the total number of subjects in the community, which is represented by N_1, we can have a measure on whether it is optimal for the state to work for the interests of all. In the current example, where S_1^1 is smaller than N_1, it is not in the best interest of the state to work for the interests of all subjects.

For the state to work for the interests of all, we need to have the optimal number of subjects for the state to work for to coincide with or be larger than the total number of subjects in the community, as represented by E_1^2 and E_1^3 in figure 14.1, with the former being the equilibrium when the marginal cost curve moves to MC_1^2 and the latter being the equilibrium when the marginal benefit curve moves to MB_1^2. As depicted, it could also be the case that the equality happens at a point beyond the total size of the community. In figure 14.2, we assume that instead of N_2^1, the size of the community is at N_2^2. At that level, the state gets a marginal benefit of MB_2^2, which is in excess of the corresponding marginal cost of MC_2^2. The state is thus incentivized to work for the interests of all (N_2^2).

Figure 14.2.

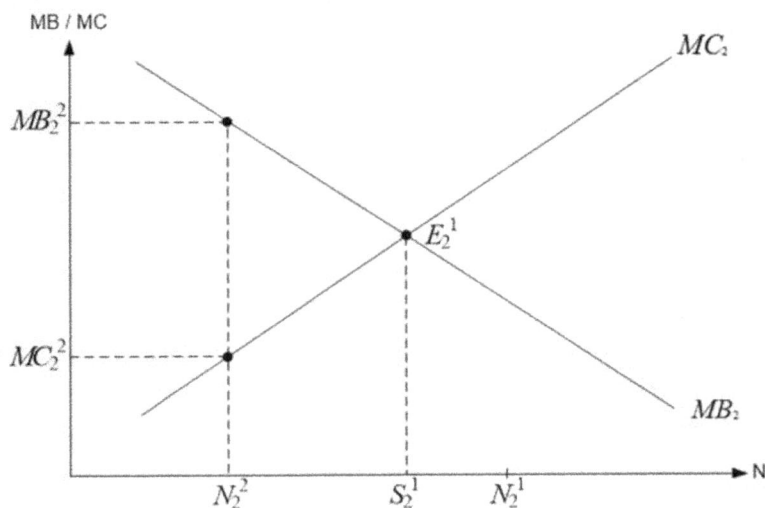

Movements of Curves

The marginal benefit and the marginal cost curves may move, which can be attributed to different causes. For instance, the state may realign its organization arrangements such that it could lower the cost of getting the support of the subjects, as shown by the downward shift of the marginal cost curve from MC_3^1 to MC_3^2 in figure 14.3.

Figure 14.3.

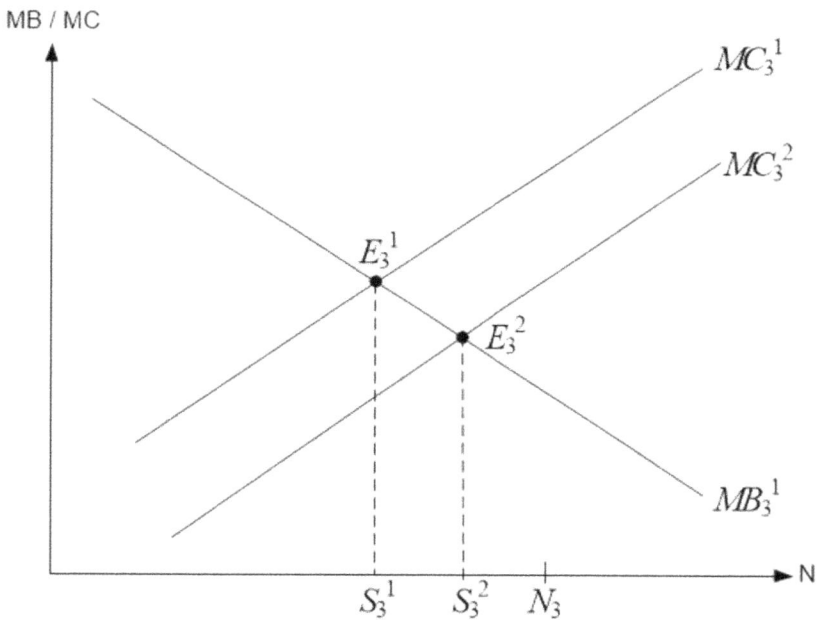

The state now finds it more beneficial to pursue the interests of more subjects (i.e., from S_3^1 to S_3^2), although it still falls short of all members of the community (i.e., N_3). Now suppose that instead of the state, perhaps based on the availability of some enhanced communications technology or the emergence of some anchorages, it is the subjects that have become more effectively organized, thereby presenting a bigger threat to the state. It becomes less beneficial for the state to concentrate on securing the support of a few cronies than getting the allegiance of the larger public. The marginal benefit curve of the state may shift accordingly, as illustrated in figure 14.4, where it moves from MB_4^1 to MB_4^2.

Figure 14.4.

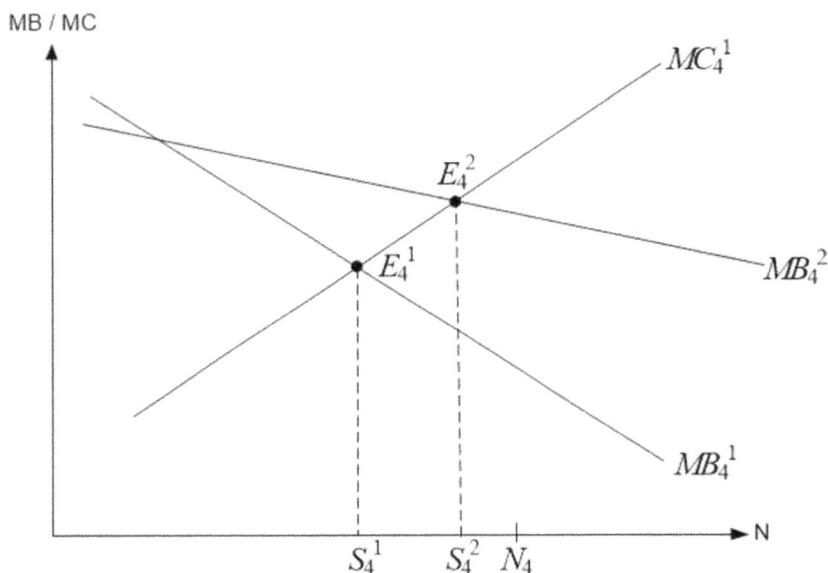

As a result, the equilibrium point shifts to E_4^2. Instead of taking care of the interests of only S_4^1 subjects, it now becomes worthwhile for the state to work for the interests of a larger group of S_4^2 subjects, though it still falls short of all members of the community as denoted by N_4.

Special Cases

The above analysis illustrates the general tendency for factional politics to emerge. Nonetheless, this does not always need to be the case. In political mechanisms where unanimous votes are required or each member has the right to veto, it becomes more likely that the marginal benefit of getting support from the electorates remains above its marginal cost throughout the size of the community. Similarly, if the state is so vulnerable that only a minute disapproval to it by the citizenry is enough to pull it from power— or if the interests of the citizenry of a community is so congenial, while not necessarily homogeneous, such that disapproval by one implies disapproval by all, and the point of change is within the maximum challenge capacity—then we may have a case where it is optimal for the incumbent state to pursue the interests of all.

Those special cases are represented by figure 14.5, where marginal benefits are zero before reaching the total number of subjects N_5, at which the marginal benefit jumps to MB^*, which also equals the total benefit.

Figure 14.5.

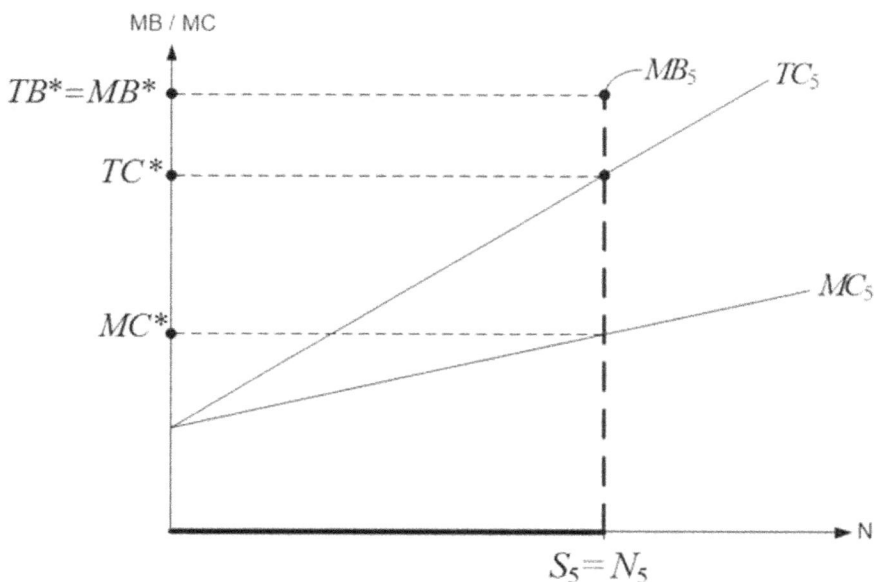

This illustrates the case where it is futile for the state to work for the interests of any portion of the citizenry other than the whole. Whether it is worthwhile for the state to stay depends on whether the total benefit at N_5 is more than the corresponding total cost as represented by the TC_5 curve.

If total benefit does exceed the total cost as in figure 14.5 (MB^* or TB^* is larger than TC^*), it is worthwhile for the state to work for the interests of all. If otherwise, then the best strategy for the state is to quit, resulting in anarchy or being taken over by a more efficient administration.

Although the above framework helps us analyze whether or not a state would work for the whole community, there is no theoretical linkage between the optimum for the state and the whole community. The model only shows where the optimum lies, and is then compared with the number of subjects in the community. There is no automatic tendency for the optimum to gravitate to the number of subjects in the community.

SUMMARY

Citing the problem of public goods, we see that the complications arising from nonexclusivity in the consumption of some goods or services can be resolved by the availability of some technical or commercial improvements, such that provisions of the goods or services via the markets become commercially viable. This does not give the state an intrinsic or inevitable role. After all, even given that there is a role for the state in the economy or the community, how can we be sure that the state will carry out the "assigned" duty? That gives us the dilemma of the state, or how to discipline the entity. The state is to pursue policies in accordance with the interests of all subjects, but remains a self-interest entity, and to carry out its duties effectively, it is coercively the strongest in the community.

To resolve the dilemma of the state, or for the state to pursue for the interests of all members of the collective (despite its being a self-interest and coercively the strongest entity), we need to have the equality of marginal benefit and marginal cost in getting support from the community members to be at or beyond the size of the community—such that it is worthwhile for the state to obtain the support of each and every one in the polity. While credible challenge by each individual member in the form of direct confrontation has been ruled out by the assumption that the state is the strongest party in the collective, disciplinary force on the state may be from coalitions of the community members. That could be due to several factors, including the presence of anchorages that can boost up the maximum challenge force, the interests of the members of the collective being very congenial, or the political mechanism being structured in such a way that disapproval by any one member is enough to defeat the incumbent.

While it is possible to effectively discipline the state to work for the interests of all subjects of the collective, these remain possibilities but not a theoretical guarantee, primarily because there are no causal dynamics linking the total number of subjects in a community to the cost-and-benefit calculus for the state to get the support of any number of the subjects. In other words, there is no force driving the equilibrium number of subjects to be served to the total number of subjects in the community.

In short, from the perspective of the expanded model, there is no mechanism that can guarantee effective choice always being exercised or the interests of every individual being protected. Different types of mechanism may have different ramifications on the benefits and costs of each individual in the community when pursuing propositions to fence or foster competition to further one's interests. In fact, the type of mechanism in place may more accurately reflect the choice of the dominant for protecting its interests.

Changes in the type of mechanism, therefore, may well be caused by changes in the dominant interests, which in turn may be precipitated by changes in the underlying interests. These then may be represented in the form of parameter changes, as we are going to discuss in the next chapter.

15

Transformation of Competition
Structures: Importance of Parameters

We have expanded the neoclassical model in which one maximizes one's benefit or profit by varying the levels of spending to fence and foster competition. In this chapter, we discuss, using a few examples, the importance of the underlying factors or parameters of the model, as they can have a significant bearing on the costs and benefits of those strategies.

COERCIVE CAPABILITY: ALEXANDER THE GREAT
As pointed out earlier, one important parameter in determining what strategies to take and their outcomes is the differentials in the coercive capabilities of the individuals concerned. The more coercively capable side is better positioned to benefit at the expense of the weaker counterparties. That means a party that commands a lead in coercive capability over its rivals is more likely to stage an aggressive campaign, actual or threatened, to capitalize on that advantage.

Major territorial expansions in history, particularly those attained within a short period of time, are often characterized by the aggressive side possessing some newly developed and overwhelming coercive capability over its rivals. The hostile maneuvers may aim, for instance, to loot or crush the competitors (i.e., reducing the competition intensity), enslave the defeated so as to enlarge the pool of subjects working for it (i.e., fostering competition on the counterparty side), or any combination of those and other tactics of similar effects.

History is filled with examples of such conquests, with one side having developed overwhelming coercive advantages over its rivals. Alexander III of Macedon (or Alexander the Great) is one of the more commonly known. The foundation of his lead in coercive might was manifold, ranging from his own genius in reading battles on the field to incentive, organizational, and weaponry changes, some introduced by his father, Philip II.

The huge treasuries looted, particularly of the Persians, filled up the war chests, which together with property and income taxes, as well as the forced contributions collected, significantly increased the gains that could be extracted from conquests. That demonstrated the huge rewards and the incentive for those who could develop coercive superiority. Fitting this back into the example used in chapter 10, the Macedon king, as an Outsider, took over and became the new Dominant.

The rise of Alexander's empire is illustrated by figure 15.1. Instead of being the king of Macedon only, as represented by N^0, the lead in coercive capabilities led to a change in an underlying factor of the costs and benefits of the strategies. The coercion lead made it less costly to expand his reign to a much larger size, shifting the marginal cost curve from MC^0 to MC^1. The optimal size of his kingdom moved from N^0 to N^1, and the total net gain also increased from AE^0B to AE^1C correspondingly.

Figure 15.1.

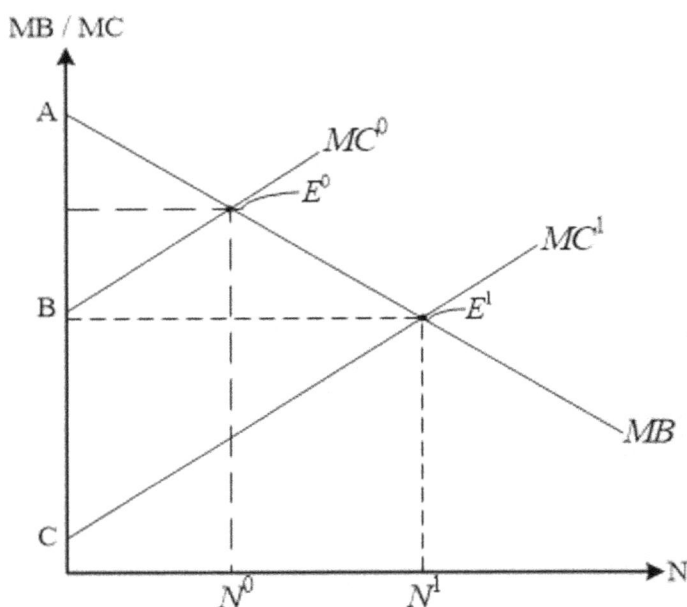

Alexander died without an heir who could be as dominant as he had been. Although the defeated Persians and other tribes could not stage a meaningful comeback, Alexander's generals turned against one another, breaking the empire apart. Their differentials in coercive abilities were insignificant, and none commanded a coercive advantage over the others. The resulting Wars of the Diadochi were inconclusive but exhaustive. Outlays on fencing and fighting drained resources. With diminished war chests, the coercive capabilities of each of the Diadochi were weakened, eventually making them unable to stem the rise of new rivals who wedged a coercive lead over them, the foremost of which were the Romans.

THE BUSINESS OF REGIMES AND PROPERTIES

The businesses of running a regime and a property are similar. Other than having a landmass or a physical property as the prerequisite for the business, the benefit-and-cost schedules applicable to a state administrator as analyzed in the expanded model also suggest a certain optimal size of landmass under its governance. This is similar to the optimal level of output for a profit-maximizing firm, property business included, where, given its production possibilities frontier, it is expected to earn the maximum profit.

In addition, the state enforces its ownership rights against intruders by means of border control and military defense. A property owner in a private property rights system relies on physical protection devices, such as locks, security systems, and fences, as well as on coercive force, including security services and judicial protection, the provision of which ultimately rests on the power of the state. Though the means are not exactly the same, the similarity is that both business types require enforceable ownership rights.

Furthermore, a property with its ownership defined implies that the nonowners are also defined. If the nonowners want to make use of the property in any way, they need to obtain the consent of the owners in whatever form is applicable. That is to say, by buying a property, the buyer is in fact acquiring the rights to admit, with or without charges, those of his or her choice to pursue activities, also of his or her choice, on the property. Thus acquiring a property under a private property rights system means acquiring the rights to fence and to foster competition on the property. Unless there are substitutes or other properties with differences the consumers find immaterial, owning a property under the private property rights system entails the owner having some extent of market power. The question for the owner, then, is whether he or she can generate satisfactory return from the rights to fence and foster competition on the property when compared with the cost of owning it.

Take a shopping-mall operator as an illustration. The operator may expand the scale of its fencing strategy by snapping up a significant portion of premises suitable for running a shopping mall in a designated area. The operator could then capture the rental income generated from making use of the acquired property by the tenants. As a condition of expansion or moving in, the mall operator may as well bargain with the authorities by demanding guarantees or the protection of not allowing other shopping-mall operators to set up business in the area to compete with it.[65]

Apart from fencing competition, the operator may also foster competition among its counterparties (i.e., the tenants). It may launch promotional campaigns or other initiatives to increase the traffic flow, such that the higher expected revenue stream would entice more prospective tenants to come to bid for retail space in the mall and existing tenants to be more willing to pay higher rents. Competition intensity among the tenants is pushed up, benefiting the mall operator.

The operator may attain the above by lowering the commuting cost for visitors to go to the property. It may also engineer economies of concentration by bringing the same groups of products under one roof. That strategy is of particular relevance for big-ticket items that are purchased only occasionally, because consumers shopping for such items are more inclined to shop around. Going to a single place where major sellers are available could save one's search costs significantly, inducing shoppers to go to a theme mall when purchasing such items. With a higher concentration of shoppers for their products, the prospective return for the tenant sellers would be enhanced as well.

However, the leeway is not always on the owner's side. Intense competition among landlords in a locality would mean that a tenant could move around without having to bear material loss of customers, particularly if a tenant is able to hook customer flows onto itself by means of, say, a strong brand name. In such cases, a mall's customer flow is raised due to the strong tenant's occupancy, so that the leeway is more on the side of the tenant, who gets some better lease terms as a result (i.e., anchor tenants).

The above are only a few possible propositions that a mall operator may pursue. Since it is the net gain that matters to each party, a property owner needs to evaluate the benefits and costs of each possible strategy. Blocking competitors from entering the markets may incur lobbying expenses. Enticing customers to come requires putting in resources. Lower

---

65 Alternatively, if it is the tenants that have the strong bargaining power, they may demand a long lock-in period with low rents in the lease contracts.

rents for anchor tenants may imply lower rental revenue. Nonetheless, such outlays or loss of revenue may be recouped by the higher rentals that can be received from, for instance, the remaining tenants who would benefit from the resulting higher traffic.[66]

Extrapolating back to the political economy arena, a state, especially an authoritarian one, may focus on the net tax revenue as much as a business on net profit. The competition for anchor tenants, for instance, mimics the competition among countries for talents by implementing targeted immigration policies, or for leading business players to establish local operations by launching correspondingly structured seed programs, development policies, or trade initiatives.[67] Running a state, particularly when viewed in the expanded model, is not that different from a running a business after all.

BUSINESS OF ACCESS

The economic value of a property is premised on the value of the activities taking place on it. One may go to a supermarket for household goods or to a boutique for clothing. For physical shelters, one could apply for public housing, rent or acquire a private flat, or in a more prehistoric notion, live in a cave. If a property houses no activity of value, not only currently but perpetually, it could hardly command any economic value.

The same rationale applies to the value of access. Whether one is willing to pay for the access to a certain destination, physical or virtual, depends firstly on whether one could derive any value from the destination and secondly on whether the net value of such is higher than the access

---

66 To capture spillover benefits other than paying lower rents, an anchor tenant or business that can steer in strong customer flows may well be incentivized to become a property owner as well.

67 Yet the lower rents offered to tenants, particularly by some local authorities in the name of development initiatives, may mask some significant costs. As a more extreme example, one may be enticed to lease land for a long time at a bargain price or even for free, only to find out, after moving in and having incurred a significant amount of relocation and setup costs, that the charges for some items typically expected to be nominal (like connection charges for electricity supply or inspection costs for meeting some safety standards) are much higher than the savings in the rent.

cost. Similar to any other business, an access business operator will evaluate whether it is in its interest to, say, fence off other accesses to the same destination or to raise the competition intensity by widening the capacity of the access to the destination.

In completely fenced-off cases, an access may be a monopoly simply because, physically or geographically, there is only one route to the destination. Or it may be under government regulatory protection (e.g., water supply). It could also be premised on the specific technical requirements of the access or distribution channels. For example, the minimum size of a shopping mall may be enough to house one hundred tenants, serving a neighborhood of two thousand households, while the minimum for an electricity network may include a million households. The incumbent may command further leeway if the cost to expand the capacity to meet the needs of additional customers after the initial threshold is negligible, while a new entrant might need to establish a completely separate infrastructure for entering the business. As such, while entry and exit are possible, given the prevailing size of the market, there may be only one operator that could be profitable.

Such leeway may well give access providers the advantage in securing correspondingly strong bargaining power on the supply side, inducing the access providers to become a supplier as well, or vice versa. That may explain why it is more difficult to make it commercially viable to forge competition by letting other suppliers plug into the network if the network operator continues to be a supplier. The distributor-supplier is incentivized and well positioned to drive out new entrants by levying, explicitly or implicitly, prohibitively high connection charges. To forcibly break up ownerships of the access and the supply businesses, particularly where the networks are available to only a handful of large suppliers, the network operator business may then become too disadvantaged to be commercially tenable.

Common examples of this include fixed-line phone operators, energy supply networks, and water supply networks. While phone connections between two parties in a locality may not be expensive, it is the connectivity to all that requires sizeable capital expenditures. Similarly, while it may be technically feasible to set up an individual home-based energy supply, say, by means of retail-size tanked gas or solar energy technologies, such business models may be driven out commercially by the economies of scale that would become more compellingly prevalent in densely popu-lated cities. The larger operators' leeway may be further strengthened by arrangements with the industry administrator, which warrants them pro-tected markets (e.g., in the form of requirement of license issued by the authorities or administrator for conducting the business) in order to, for instance, induce them to enter the business or build a more enduring col-lusion among the administrator and the selected privileged factions to sus-tain the rule and governance of the administrator.

Unless an entrant is confident in displacing the incumbent or taking a large enough market share from it, the prospective return to build an alternative access in an area that has only the minimum size of users may not look promising, particularly for products where access is not charged separately. The chance of having an alternative access provider in such a market is therefore correspondingly low, resulting in a fenced-off market.

The competition landscape of an access business, however, may be fun-damentally changed by the availability of alternative access technologies that give rise to very different fencing and fostering cost-benefit calculi. The size of gains that could be collected from a certain strategy mix for some of the parties may be curtailed, while that for others may be in-creased. For example, the importance of the trading and servicing points on the Silk Road (as the then major access between the East and the West) dwindled when sea transport became commercially viable and increasingly large scale and sophisticated. Nevertheless, when air transport asserted its dominance, the economic value of some key seaports also became supple-mental, particularly for items where timeliness and speediness of delivery were of a high value. New technology may also torpedo the circumscribing efficiency of an incumbent and raise its fencing cost significantly, as the following discussion on the effects that the spread of Internet access and digital technology has on the music records business illustrates.

THE CASE OF RECORD LABELS

Music record label companies are essentially holders of the distribution rights of music productions. As the production of the musical pieces and the subsequent mass replications of the master records onto whatever the distribution medium currently in widespread commercial use (like cassettes, vinyl discs, compact discs, or encrypted files) may be subcontracted to corresponding production and manufacturing facilities, the record label companies are primarily engaged in reselling the acquired rights in different forms. They may also be managers or agents of the artists, representing them in negotiating and overseeing the execution of the reselling of copyrights and other commercial contracts like promotion events, performances, and advertising contracts.

To generate commercial value, music pieces need to be distributed to buyers. Before the Internet became a distribution channel, a consumer needed to buy the pieces copied onto a physical medium and have a corresponding device (like a cassette player, tuner, or CD player) to play them on. For cassette and vinyl discs, reproduction by one's own means is technically feasible but not commercially viable on a large scale, constituting an effective fencing barrier in favor of the copyright holders. The fencing efficiency, however, is compromised when CD burners are available for retail uses, such that larger-scale commercial reproduction operating on a dispersed network mode is viable at a low cost. Here, pirated copies began to take away a significant share of the total market.

The onset of Internet distribution via media files, such that distributions to those connected could be executed simply by mouse clicks, dealt an even heavier blow to the fencing effectiveness of the recording industry. This gave the electronic dissemination model a surpassing advantage over incumbent distribution channels.

One-Man Band

Internet distribution has also hit the record labels on another front. Large labels, which could diversify risks by means of establishing a large portfolio of distribution rights and afford launching promotion campaigns, usually can leverage their size to secure their share of shelf space at retail shops. For the lesser-known artists, in contrast, given their lack of a proven track record of sales, retail shops and other media like radio stations are typically unwilling to allocate their limited shelf space or broadcast time to those artists for the higher risk involved.

While it is possible for a recording artist to take on the whole workflow, from composing to selling the records, the above suggests that the cost-benefit matrix in the industry incentivizes artists to contract with the large record labels, further strengthening the latter's advantage in the competition, and wedging the cost of access to consumers against those lesser-known artists.

Internet distribution, however, has remarkably lowered the access cost for artists and consumers. The low cost of putting one's productions onto the Internet helps the lesser-known artists bypass the label companies and retail shops to distribute their pieces and, with the wider availability of the corresponding payment-collection technology, collect revenue for their productions. They can also build up their commercial credibility to solicit other opportunities like distribution in other media as well as performances in terms of shows and concerts. Established artists may also take this as an alternative channel to distribute their productions on top of the record labels' traditional channels, if they have not bypassed the record labels altogether.

Dwindling Fencing Efficiency

The extensiveness and the sheer size of the Internet audience suggest that it is costly to set up and implement fencing of comparable efficiency and profitability as in the past. For instance, the cost of establishing and enforcing an effective worldwide legal framework against unauthorized distributions on the web is prohibitive relative to the economic value of each case.

The more effective means of fencing in this case would be via enhancements of the encryption and payment-collection technologies. Yet while that may prevent illegal distributions from taking up an even larger share of the market, the threat of Internet distribution over traditional distribution channels is unlikely to recede. One would expect that evolving electronic media will be increasingly dominant in the distribution of or access to authorized music records.

In the new arena, portals that could facilitate shoppers getting what they want swiftly and cost-effectively could command a competitive edge. The same is true for manufacturers of the devices capable of playing the records, as those manufacturers evidently may also try to capitalize on their established access to buyers to become competing portals.

The record labels are forced to recalibrate their fencing-fostering mix in the face of the Internet challenge. With a lower fencing efficiency in the traditional distribution channels, the labels are more inclined to join the competition on the new platform. Capitalizing on their voluminous record libraries, the record labels enjoy some incumbent advantages that can help them establish a foothold in the new virtual arena by forming their own music download business, in effect selling prosecution-free licenses. The competition landscape is also being shaped by those high-traffic portals that may capitalize on traffic flow to foster competition among the record labels. The determinant of success would likely be on the abilities to leverage consumers' inertia in shifting to a new platform, which in turn originates from the tendency to save or to avoid incurring search costs.

* * *

The examples discussed in this chapter illustrate the importance of the underlying parameters, as those can have a strong bearing on the cost-and-benefit calculi of the parties concerned. A change in relative coercive capabilities may lead to emergence of a new dominant player. The viability and relevance of the incentive structures of how a property complex, or a state, is managed might determine the profitability and sustainability of the property or the administration, particularly when the economic or technological (including coercive) challenges facing it change. Onsets of new technologies may have different ramifications on the efficiencies of the different parties' strategies to fence and foster competition and can redraw the business landscape.

16

Reinterpreting the Neoclassical Model

The rigor of the competitive equilibrium under the neoclassical model is premised on individual choice. Each individual chooses what is best for him or her. As such, under the model, exchanges are mutually beneficial, and individual optima coincide with the social optimum. However, as shown in the expanded model, that is not always the case when compared with the status quo. In this chapter, we further elaborate on the implications that the expanded model has on the key concepts of the neoclassical model.

The expanded model rests on relaxing the assumption that no individual is allowed to inflict harm on others. When harming others is allowed, it may well be in the rational interests of an individual to restrain the effective choice domain of others or enlarge his or her own domain by fencing or fostering competition, respectively. That is, competition intensity becomes a choice variable in an individual's decision analysis but not a given parameter as assumed in the neoclassical model. To mimic the maximum competition intensity as stipulated under the perfect competition setting, we need to have the fencing option not chosen and the fostering option always exercised to the fullest, which can be attained by the fulfillment of the following two conditions for each and every individual in a community:

1. The fencing option is always not preferred (i.e., marginal benefit of fencing always equals or is less than the marginal cost, even when fencing spending is zero).

2. There is no more possible gain from fostering competition (i.e., marginal benefit from fostering competition has become equal to or less than the marginal cost after a certain positive amount of spending on fostering competition).[68]

Under the above conditions, no one willing to enter the market, whether as a buyer or a seller, would be blocked from doing so, and whenever there is perceived gain from fostering competition, individuals would do so to seize it, resulting in new competition joining the markets. Market dynamics under such conditions replicate that in the perfect competition setting in the neoclassical model, except we do not need to have numerous sellers and buyers.

THE CHOICE VARIABLES

By changing the choice variable from the quantity of a good in the neoclassical utility-maximization model for a consumer, and the quantities of labor and capital in the profit-maximization model for a firm, to spending to fence and foster competition, the corresponding solutions reflect not only the resulted quantities and prices in the respective models but also the consequential effects on competition intensity. Furthermore, competition intensity, as commonly represented by the different discrete types of market structure (namely, perfect competition, monopolistic competition, oligopoly, and monopoly, each of which constituting a certain level of competition intensity) and as an independent concept in the neoclassical model becomes a continuum.

---

68 The situation where there are numerous sellers and only one dominant buyer, with all of the former living on subsistence, is a good example of no more expected gain from fostering competition for the buyer. In such cases, there is in effect no alternative buyer who would help the sellers to build up their bargaining power. As in the case of the Roman Empire, the lesser subjects became so impoverished that they did not have either the capital or (given the expectation that all gains would be extracted) the incentive to raise their productivity. The gross reward for the dominant in such a situation is likely to be abnormally high, as evidenced by the wealth accumulated by the nobles. The fencing costs against outside challenges to take the place of the incumbent dominant and against the subjects from competing against one another would also be high.

In addition, while the number of players could have a bearing on the intensity of competition, it is not the definitive variable on the level of competition intensity being maintained in the traditional market-structure theory. Market structure or competition intensity is the result of individual rational choices concerning fencing and fostering strategies, with the distribution of their capabilities in the respective fields being the more significant factors.

COMPLETE APPROPRIATION

For the market system to function well, complete definition and appropriation of property rights to each piece of property is needed. Gains could be made if the definition of property rights in an incomplete system is improved. That suggests that the scale of the latent gains that could be uncovered may reflect the extent of changes that the antimarket strategies pursued by individuals may have generated if the misappropriation was a result of those strategies.

Why is that the case? To maximize one's net gain, one may pursue fencing or fostering strategies to distort the property rights system or make it more inefficient or incomplete if doing so is the best option available to them. For instance, keeping the property rights regime clumsy, complicated, and "costly" may be the deliberate strategy pursued by the bureaucracy to make others to pay them to get through the bottlenecks or roadblocks they have enacted. If the red tape is removed, the consideration formerly paid to them would stay with the citizenry.

Similarly, to lure in investments, a local administration may knowingly disregard the pollution effects that a manufacturing process may bring on the poorer subjects in the locality. By not appropriating the damages on the residents as a cost to the investors, the local authorities are in effect subsidizing the latter at the expense of the former—or transferring, wholly or partially, resources from poorer subjects to the investing entrepreneurs and the authorities themselves.

Fencing or fostering competition may take the form of distorting the appropriation of costs and benefits among the parties concerned to one's advantage or benefit, especially to those who are dominant. Pursuits to promote or to impede the smooth functioning of the market mechanism are both strategic options integral to one's choice domain.

EFFECTIVE CHOICE

The above highlights the importance of the choice domain in the robustness of individual choice. When evaluating the virtues and vices of the market system versus, for instance, the communist planned model, the freedom to choose obviously takes a high priority. However, without meaningful choices available, the freedom to choose alone may not bring us any material benefit. Corresponding fencing and fostering strategies as executed by the dominant—whether an individual, corporate entity, or an authority—may well consign the lesser subjects to a state of impoverished and deprived as in a communist planned country, even if they are living in a market democracy with each endowed with full-fledged freedom.

It is true that the chance that exchanges are mutually beneficial is higher as competition intensifies, but that remains a probabilistic premise and cannot be taken for certainty. The disadvantaged may still find themselves locked in a pool of negative propositions when compared with the status quo, like working for subsistence wages, confiscations of properties, imprisonment, or death. Even the best offer may be a negative proposition. The key issue is whether the dominant players can be disciplined by competition, bringing us back to the extreme case of the dilemma of the state, where the most powerful entity in a collective is to be disciplined to pursue the interests of the subjects. Although the conditions conducive to the effective disciplining of the strongest entity and hence having effective choice by all can be specified, they fall short of a guarantee.

OPTIMA

The concept of "optimum" in economics is based on the notion of Pareto improvement, which is where a change brings forth improvement in the well-being of some with none being worse off. A variation to this is if some parties are made worse off by the change but compensated by those better off, directly or indirectly, such that the compensated are at least as well off as before and the beneficiary parties could still reap gains after paying the compensation. When all possible gains are exhausted and there is no more Pareto improvement, every individual of the collective is at his or her respective optimum state, or the Pareto optimum.

With the collective being the aggregation of individuals, when there is no more possible gain at the individual level, there could also be no more possible gain to the social well-being.[69] That is, when each and every individual is at the optimum, the collective must also be at the best possible state or the optimum, resulting in the individual optima coinciding with the social optimum.

However, that brings us to a number of questions. The above is rested on the assumption that each individual is rational (where more of a good is preferred to less) and able to cling on to the status quo, such that when one accepts a change, it is not a worse-off move. We have seen, however, that if an individual is unable to defend his or her status quo, then that is no guarantee as to whether that individual will not become worse off after a change.

What we can say is that a rational individual will choose the best options available to him or her. If he or she is presented with an assortment of options that are all inferior to his or her status quo and the option of the status quo is also not available, then he or she will choose the "least bad" option. Since he or she will still be at the best possible state, he or she will be at a new individual optimum—which, however, is worse than the previous one.

The same is true on the social level: with no more feasible options that could improve the state of the collective, the collective is also said to be at the social optimum. Whether the new social optimum is better than the previous one is uncertain and depends on whether the aggregated gains attributable to those who benefit from the change are larger than the aggregate losses borne by those who suffer. In case the aggregate gain falls

---

69 For that to be true, we need to assume that the cost to search for possible improvements by each individual with every other individual is negligible.

short of the aggregate loss, we will have a non-Pareto change that brings us from one set of optima to another. Even if we have the aforementioned conditions fulfilled such that the maximum intensity of competition is in place, then this still does not guarantee that the status quo is an option and that a change is always a Pareto improvement.

If we cannot be sure that any change is a Pareto improvement, we can only maintain the argument that rational behavior of a self-interest individual would bring the collective to the best possible state, but the new best possible state may be worse than the previous one. However, when at the new set of optima, we will also have no more possible improvements, implying that state is a Pareto optimum as well. That is, we can move from one Pareto optimum to another by means of a non-Pareto improvement change.[70]

The above, in effect, pushes the neoclassical model's thesis that exchanges are always mutually beneficial and lead to improvements in social well-being—which is already a special case where the conditions specifying the model need to be met to become a more stringent special case. We can only spell out the conditions where the chance of having that is higher—or, more specifically, the conditions that would raise the intensity of competition such that the dominant, including the state, will be subject to more effective disciplinary forces. However, without the status-quo option, the preceding does not warrant the validity of the thesis that exchanges are always mutually beneficial versus the parties' level of well-being before the exchanges.

---

70 Alternatively speaking, Pareto optimum is more of a snapshot concept, or the best possible state given prevailing conditions or cost-and-benefit calculi of members of the community. It carries no ontological meaning or track record comparison, such that it does not have the meaning of "better." However, that is in marked contrast with the notions of harmony and progress associated with the optimum concept.

17

Changing the Dominant
Theses and Society

Applications of the expanded model are not limited to economic issues. This can indeed be applied to any issues involving choices, which could be represented as a problem of choice over different and competing theses.

FORMATION OF DOMINANT THESES

The dominant thesis for any issue, simply put, is the proposition that is adopted. The underlying interests that put up the dominant thesis or the interests that benefit from that thesis are deemed as the dominant interests. The issue could be on allocation, which may be between two brothers over who has an apple, among the customers in a marketplace over the apples put on sale, or among the wholesalers over the distribution rights of apples in a country. It could also be about a position, such as who is to be the treasurer of a student association, financial controller of a company, or the treasury secretary of a nation. As long as there is more than one individual or party interested in the item, we have an allocation issue and need a corresponding thesis to resolve it (i.e., to determine how to allocate the item in question).

A simple thesis to allocate the apple between the two brothers could be: whoever does the cleanup work gets the apple. For the apples in the market, paying the displayed price usually gets you one, as long as stock lasts. For the national distribution rights, they may be allocated via an open auction or a tender process. As for who is to be the officer on financial matters, that could be decided by a simple vote among the members of the group concerned, or by appointment by the head of the organization in question.

However, there may be alternative theses, conceivable or proposed, and the parties interested in the issue may not reach an agreement that readily over which thesis is to be used for resolving the allocation matter (i.e., who decides which thesis should be used to allocate the apples or pick who is to be the officer on treasury matters). Yet there has to be only one dominant thesis in place or else the allocation issue will become a dispute, which may need to be resolved a level up, or by the parties that those who are in dispute agree to appeal to. Would that be, say, the boys' father, the store manager, the government, or the chairman of the executive committee?

Evidently, disputes can be escalated further if no agreement can be made at that higher level. For instance, in case the legitimacy of a vote by the executive committee members is challenged, the issue may be raised up to the level of the school principal, or voting by all the students of the school. If that is still not enough to resolve the dispute, decisions by the school management board may be needed. It is conceivable, though not likely in practice, that the disputes could be pushed further upward to a level that is beyond the school, especially if the disputes are about who has the ultimate authority to determine the rules for settling disputes or which thesis is to be adopted as the dominant one.

Settlement

For a dispute to be settled, we need the concerned parties to find it in their interests to comply with the adoption of a certain proposition as the dominant thesis, or in their interests not to oppose the adoption of that proposition. To arrive at such an accord, the benefit of adopting that thesis for the consenting parties will have to exceed the cost of complying with it—or in the case that adopting that thesis brings forth a loss when compared with the status quo, that the loss is less than the cost of not adopting the thesis. If there are still parties not willing to conform to the thesis adopted or to be adopted, we need to have that the cost that their noncompliance poses on others is insufficient to derail the adoption of the thesis. The thesis that can achieve that or that could most closely achieve that becomes the dominant thesis.

In a market economy, the typical dominant thesis determining allocation is the price mechanism. Whoever is willing and able to pay the asking price (which could be the highest bid price in an auction, the specified price on the price tag in a supermarket, and the like) can buy the item being put on for sale. The same is applicable if you are a seller. If powerful enough, a seller may set or amend the allocation rule for its counterparties to follow. For example, a grocery store may accept cash payments only or charge extra for payments in credit cards. A machine manufacturer might require payment in advance of production.

Allocation problems obviously are not confined to the market economy. To win a seat in a political body in a democracy, one needs to secure the corresponding number of votes in an election. To obtain basic necessities in a communist planned model, a peasant may have to comply with the requirements prescribed by the party but subject to the interpretations and executions by the local comrades who are the actual dominant entity in a locality. The set requirements may not be in terms of the volume of produce to be submitted only but on political, communal, and familial matters as well.

DOMINANT INTERESTS

The preceding shows that the dominant thesis in place (e.g., highest bidder, highest number of votes won, or meeting the requirements prescribed by the comrades) also stipulates the parties that constitute the dominant interests (i.e., those who pay the highest price and those who have the goods for sale to the highest bidder; those who have won the highest number of votes and the electors voting for the winners; and the local comrades and those who could most meet their demands). It could be the interests of the dominant party (e.g., the local comrades) or a group of parties that together become the dominant entity (e.g., the consumers and the voters).

Other than the consumers and the voters, another example of individual interests becoming the dominant when aggregated would be the basketball fans who together are the de facto dominant interests for the basketball business. For a correspondingly gifted boy who wants to pursue a career as a basketball player in a market economy, he has to win a place on a professional team by showing his capability in not only winning the games for the team, but probably also in appealing to the basketball fans, especially if he wants to secure a contract of a higher commercial value. In contrast, if he is in the national team of an authoritarian country, he may need to show his ability to win the games and, more importantly, the will to comply with the state's directives, because it is the authoritarian state that is the dominant interest.

Take the media industry as a further example. Newspapers owned by the state apparatus in an authoritarian regime are typically a propaganda tool used by the state to secure and sustain its rule. Even if non-state-owned media operations are allowed, their reach and influence are likely to be managed and contained. For media businesses in a liberal society where citizenry interests are diverse and competing, the market players are likely to represent or carry those different political interests or affiliations, with their circulations likely to resemble the corresponding distribution of political interests and affiliations in the society, after adjusting for differences in purchasing power for media services.

EVOLUTION OF THE SOCIETY

Although a dominant thesis can be displaced, it is not cost free to do so. One may need to lobby for a change to obtain the needed support or may need to stage a military campaign to unseat an incumbent. The higher or the more levels that may need to be appealed to or resorted to, the more costly the displacement would be. This, in effect, endows the incumbent an advantage in preventing it from being replaced. The more costly it is to displace it, the greater the advantage the incumbent would have.

That bias also implies that propositions that comply with or are in line with the incumbent thesis are more likely to be pursued. This not only sustains the thesis but also discourages the use of competing alternatives. For instance, choice in the market system is made with regard to preferences as expressed in the prices paid and that in democracy, as practiced so far, by the number of votes. The use of the price system means that goods and services are to go to the highest bidder, but not to, say, the party who wins a fight. Democracy, as the institutionalized way for replacing or retaining the ruling party, minimizes the chance of (and the associated loss from) bloodshed or civil war when deciding who will assume power. With the use of force being relegated, that would support the evolution of the society on the more peaceful trail. However, by the same token, if the dominant thesis is that the use of force (e.g., rifle power) is legitimate, such that the cost of staging conflicts is comparatively low, then one would expect that it is more unlikely to have a peaceful civil society.

While it is already not cost free to displace an incumbent, the dominant may even make it more costly. Typically, to enforce conformity is given a high priority. Theses of such and with long-lasting effects on the evolution path may be instilled. For instance, the state usually has the final say in the design of the education system, if not directly administering it, in order to imbue conformist values deemed important into the curricula and the minds of the future generations. Social or religious practices can also have a strong influence on not only what is regarded as "normal" but also what is "deviant." If such is enforced with the coercive power of the administration, one may be jailed or detained for defiance. Expectedly, to protect the community from breaking down or breaking up, the state would enact heavy sentences against deviances and subversions.

Continuity and Diversity

It can be also inferred that the higher the cost to displace an incumbent, the more stable the corresponding community or the grouping would be. It is more likely that propositions of alternatives are fringed out by the incumbent or dominant thesis. However, there are trade-offs. Diversity is compromised, and it is more likely that more extreme means would be adopted when staging challenges. In contrast, diversity is expected to be more vigorous if a mechanism with a low displacement cost is taken as the dominant thesis.

Alternatively speaking, the higher the level a thesis is about or the more extensive the coverage the thesis has (such as the choice over the type of political system or economic system to be adopted for the whole society), the more costly it will be to change it. As such, changes are less likely when the thesis is at a higher level or having a more extensive coverage. That, in turn, brings us to the question of whether we shall have a system that is less costly to replace an incumbent for theses at a higher level or with a more extensive coverage so as to counterbalance the typically higher replacement cost associated.

That, however, is a choice over continuity and change. Parties that prefer clinging to the status quo would like to have a system that is costly for changes to take place, while those who envisage "better alternatives" would fight for putting in a system that is conducive to changes, at least before their "alternatives" could assume dominance. In short, the choice over the type of thesis to be adopted is merely another battlefield for individuals who are pursuing propositions to fence or to foster competition.

Deemed and Genuine Dominant Interests

While the above is mainly about what is likely to happen under a certain dominant thesis, it has been implicitly assumed that the interests deemed as dominant by the dominant thesis are the same or not in conflict with the genuine underlying dominant interests of the collective. If the interests deemed dominant by the dominant thesis (or the parties that are regarded and rewarded as the winning parties under that thesis) are different from the genuine dominant interests in the collective, the latter may well topple the deemed dominant interests or even the dominant thesis altogether. That is particularly likely when a dominant thesis is newly adopted.

For example, if a government elected under a democracy being put into place not long ago is not from the incumbent dominant interests of the society, like the long-entrenched politico-military complex, a forced-upon replacement of the elected government is likely, as exemplified by the many short-lived administrations elected under infant democracies.

VARIABILITY IN WHAT IS VALUABLE

Since it is not cost free to replace an incumbent and a dominant thesis could have ramifications on the path a collective takes, the "contents" of the dominant thesis, as embedded in the preference set of each of the parties involved, play an important role. However, as in the neoclassical model or the expanded model developed here, individual preference is taken as given. Its determination is largely a black box. The effects of the "contents" of the preferences are ignored or assumed to be immaterial. An individual preferring to have an apple or undertaking murderous crimes makes no difference under the model.

Rationality only stipulates that an individual will pursue what is evaluated as the best for himself or herself after comparing the various options available. Its application does not require making assumptions on the "contents" of his or her preference or what he or she regards as valuable and not. In addition, the usual practice of taking the goods in question as the proxy of deriving satisfaction or utility has given economics a materialistic tone. It has been customarily assumed that taking (whether by paying, seizing, or other means) and consuming the goods is the purpose of economic life.

Yet the model can accommodate other denominations of what is regarded as valuable or what is unacceptable. Satisfaction may be derived from not only what one gets but also from what one gives, as well as what one does and even what one does to others. Benefit-and-cost schedules of the members of a community may change accordingly, consequently altering the strategies that they are to adopt. For instance, one may think of harming others as an unforgivable wrongdoing and attach an overwhelmingly high negative value to the pursuits of such propositions so that it is always not worthwhile to pursue them. One may also regard his or her satisfaction as being higher if the well-being of another individual, or a group of individuals, is improved. If that requires an outlay of resources, such pursuits are subject to his or her budget constraint, just like any other "normal" economic behavior as analyzed under the neoclassical model. That is, one's capacity in benevolent activities is also subject to a budget constraint; one simply cannot donate more than what one has.

Determinism or Free Will

Even after taking out the status-quo option and allowing the pursuits of harming others to benefit oneself (as having options does not necessarily mean they are being pursued), the rationality postulate imposes no restrictions on what one regards as valuable and not. We are what we do, and we have a choice in it.

That carries a connotation that is in marked contrast with the generally deterministic tone imbued in economic theories constructed on the "scientific" approach. In typical analyses of human behavior under such theories or models, predictability is a predominant criterion in assessing their usefulness or value, which in turn is founded on making some stability or fixity assumptions on human behavior or nature. That leads to the deterministic implications on human behavior, and poses stark dilemmas against the free-will arguments. If human behavior is all-predictable, how is it possible and meaningful that we have free will?

Nonetheless, by building different types of behavioral traits into the preference set or the "contents" of individual preference, or what one regards as valuable or not, human behavior is predictable only within the assumed settings and conditions. The possibilities on the types of behavioral traits that can be built into the model are not restricted. In this end, the free-will stance becomes compatible with the deterministic working of the model that is largely concerned with what happens after the assumed behavioral traits are incorporated into the preference set. Both free will and freedom of choice are fundamental building blocks in the neoclassical model.

18

Conclusion

The neoclassical model as represented by the individual optimization problem derives a number of robust and ideologically appealing conclusions, accounting for its wide applicability in microeconomics. Under the model, pursuit of one's own interests by each and every individual in the collective results in changes that are mutually beneficial or at least detrimental to none, and brings each individual and the collective, as an aggregation of individuals, to the respective best possible states. This also relieves the government from taking on an interventionist role. It is at best an administrator of the property rights system and any other supplementary mechanisms to facilitate market exchanges to take place.

However, the "best" does not necessarily mean "better" than the status quo or at what position he or she originally is in. For the model to have the notion of "betterment" or "progress," status quo needs to be assumed upheld as the floor in an individual's choice domain.

The model developed in this book expands on the neoclassical model by relaxing that underlying assumption: that the option of status quo is always available. Without that option as the floor, the whole arsenal of strategies for harming others to benefit oneself is open for choice. Instead of accepting only positive-yielding options, as compared with the status quo, one may have to face situations where only options that are worse than the individual's current state of being are available.

By choosing the "least bad" option, one is forgoing the other ones; these are not only bigger negatives, but the next "least bad" option has also become the opportunity cost for choosing the least bad. When deducting a negative figure by a numerically larger negative figure, that choice is still a beneficial one in net terms. Yet that is not a move that brings the individual to a better state when compared with the status quo. The option of the "least bad" is a net beneficial choice only in the sense that it is better than the second-least bad but not an improvement over the status quo. Choosing that option does not bring forth any benefit to the individual—it only inflicts the least harm.

Building upon the relaxed assumption, the expanded model replaces the decision variable in the optimization problem from the quantity of a good to the levels of spending needed to fence and foster competition intensity. One chooses the best mix of strategies to fence and foster competition in order to pursue what one thinks as the best for himself or herself. Taking into account each participant's capability in altering the competition intensity and aggregating the consequential interactions among them gives the equilibrium level of competition intensity and the distributions of the gains and costs among the individuals concerned.

Since benefiting oneself at the expense of others is made an option by relaxing the status-quo assumption, we can no longer be sure that exchanges are always mutually beneficial (when compared with the status-quo). Individuals may fence or foster competition intensity, or pursue a combination of both strategies, to harm others in order to benefit themselves. Worse, the more imbalanced or polarized a community is, the more likely the repressed are locked in the deprived position. Also, the more coercively capable an individual is, the more likely it is for him or her to adopt a harm-to-benefit strategy.

When the expanded model is applied to the problem of the state, it is assumed to be neither benevolent nor evil by nature. It is also not an impartial administrator of, say, the property rights system. It is assumed to be just like any other individual in a community: it pursues its self-interest and deploys all the necessary means to its benefit. By further assuming that the self-interest state is coercively the most capable—which is a prerequisite for it to enforce its rule effectively—the state is in effect made the best positioned and the most likely entity to wage aggression and force its interests onto others.

While it is possible to discipline the state to pursue the interests of the members of the community, we can only identify the type of factors that would make that more likely. To have a society free of such aggressions, we need to have a balanced distribution of bargaining capabilities that may spring from a balanced distribution of wealth, expertise in demand, coercive force, and the like. However, there are no internal dynamics that drive the state to be fully disciplined or make the society a collective of harmonious or truly mutually beneficial engagements only.

Evidently, if the repressed subjects are so impoverished that they cannot afford anything but bare necessities, or the state or the dominant interests are so compellingly powerful like the goods on offer being all owned by them, there may not be any conflict. Antagonistic parties may find it not worth the cost to bring a dispute to surface to resolve it. It could be because there is too low of an economic value at stake or that the two parties are so polarized and the disparity in coercive capability between them is so high that it is too costly for the disadvantaged side to make its claims. With antagonisms made latent, no direct and immediate threat is posed to the stability of the political entity.

However, this does not imply that the community is in harmony. The choice domain, or what one can really choose, matters just as much as the freedom to choose and the choice mechanism that can be made nominal in effect and can hardly improve the well-being of the subjects.

What is deemed as valuable in a community, or what is associated with a high value, may be a consequence of what is regarded as such by the dominant party or the members of the collective showing the same choice and turning out to be the dominant group or interests when aggregated. Put simply, the dominant thesis may be from the dominant party or the dominant aggregate. Given that it would not be cost free to replace an incumbent, the community members would in turn be incentivized to pursue a similar course.

Prejudices are not intrinsic but adopted. If a society regards, say, holding discriminatory views or bullying others as normal or tolerable (such as no one would come out to stand against it), the corresponding cost of doing that becomes lower, thereby encouraging individuals to pursue it. In contrast, if helping others or adopting a more embracive attitude toward the unfortunate or underprivileged is not regarded as an oddity but normalcy, we would expect acting as such to be more common.

Harming others for one's own benefit is made an option in the expanded model. Yet adopting this is not an unavoidable decision, even within the apparently mechanistic construct of the neoclassical model. It depends on what is regarded as valuable and what is detestable. Rewards from one's pursuits may not always be in monetary terms or exclusively in monetary terms. It could be satisfaction when aspirations are met, such as attainment of individual goals, making others happy, and the like. Value is a variable and an open choice for and by the members of the society. There is no inevitability in the decision to hate or strike; that can only be endorsed or embraced.

When virtues are adopted as the dominant theses, the issue of containing the vices of the dominant may become redundant. However, while that is a possible route to a benign society, before getting there, we still need institutional arrangements as safeguards to constrain the dominant from leveraging on its dominance to take advantage of the lesser by incentivizing effective and meaningful choice for all. As such, mechanisms or theses that enshrine choice and diversity over conformity and continuity shall be preferred. As such, even if the outcomes remain the same for a sustained period of time, it is the result of the members of the collective making the same choices over and over again. The continuity is a consequence of their making their own choices consistently, but not because of the same choices being continuously made for them. The apparent outcomes might be the same, but the route that leads to those outcomes matters more.

Bibliography

Barzel, Y. *A Theory of the State.* Cambridge: Cambridge University Press, 2002.

Friedman, M. *Capitalism and Freedom.* Chicago: The University of Chicago Press, 1982.

Mueller, D. C. *Public Choice III.* Cambridge: Cambridge University Press, 2003.

Sharma, M., G. Inchauste, and J. Feng. "Rising Inequality with High Growth and Falling Poverty." *An Eye on East Asia and Pacific, World Bank.* Washington, DC: World Bank, 2011, no. 9, 1–6 (http://documents.worldbank.org/curated/en/2011/01/14964250/rising-inequality-high-growth-falling-poverty).

Smith, A. *The Wealth of Nations.* New York: Bantam Dell, 2003.

www.ingramcontent.com/pod-product-compliance
Lightning Source LLC
Chambersburg PA
CBHW021556210326
41599CB00010B/471